Perl/Tk
Pocket Reference

Perl/Tk
Pocket Reference

Stephen Lidie

O'REILLY®

Beijing • Cambridge • Farnham • Köln • Paris • Sebastopol • Taipei • Tokyo

Perl/Tk Pocket Reference

by Stephen Lidie

Copyright © 1998 O'Reilly & Associates, Inc. All rights reserved.
Printed in the United States of America. Published by O'Reilly &
Associates, Inc., 101 Morris Street, Sebastopol, CA 95472.

Editor: Gigi Estabrook

Production Editor: Paula Carroll

Production Services: Omegatype

Cover Design: Edie Freedman and Kathleen Wilson

Printing History:

      October 1998:   First Edition

1-56592-517-3
[C]

Table of Contents

Perl/Tk Pocket Reference

Introduction

Perl/Tk is the extension to Perl for creating graphical user interfaces. This small book presents every Perl/Tk graphical element, including general widget and variable information, callbacks, geometry management, bindings, events, window management, as well as composite widget, font, and image creation and manipulation commands, all of which are described in detail in O'Reilly & Associates' *Learning Perl/Tk*.

I am very grateful to Achim Bohnet, who tenaciously reviewed this work as it evolved.

Conventions

`fixed`	denotes text that you enter literally
italics	means variable text, i.e., things you must fill in
bold	is a keyword, i.e., a word with a special meaning
?...?	denotes an optional part

1. General Perl/Tk Widget Information

All Perl/Tk programs must have a **use Tk** statement. To use special Perl/Tk widgets like **Dialog** a **use Tk::Dialog** statement is required.

All widgets are created with:

> $*widget* = $*parent* -> *widgetClass*(?-*option* => *value*, ...?);

where *widgetClass* is the name of the class of widget desired (e.g., **Button**) and $parent is the Perl/Tk widget reference of the new widget's parent. The Perl object reference is stored in $*widget*, which becomes a child of $*parent*, creating the widget hierarchy.

All widget creation commands can have the optional **Name** => *resourceName* parameter to associate a resource database name with the widget.

Every Perl/Tk program requires a main window, the topmost widget in the hierarchy, created with:

$*mw* = **MainWindow**->**new**;

The following command creates a new button widget $*b* and uses the **grid** geometry manager to map it:

$*b* = $*mw*->**Button**(-text => "Hello World")->**grid**;

Widget configuration options may be passed in the creation method. Options begin with a "-" and are usually followed by a value: an integer or string, sometimes a Perl scalar, array, hash, or code reference. After creation, options may be changed using the **configure** widget command:

$*widget*->**configure**(*-option* => *value*, ...);

and queried using the **cget** command:

$*widget*->**cget**(*-option*);

The last statement in a Perl/Tk program calls **MainLoop** to initiate event processing.

Perl/Tk Callbacks

A callback is a scalar, either a code reference or a method name as a string. Either of these styles can take parameters by passing an array reference with the code reference or method name as the first element, and subroutine parameters as subsequent elements.

\&*subroutine*   [\&*subroutine* ?, *args*?]

sub {...}   [**sub** {...} ?, *args*?]

'*methodName*'   ['*methodName*' ?, *args*?]

Note that **bind** *callbacks* are implicitly passed the bound object as the first argument of the parameter list. Refer to the section *Bindings and Virtual Events* for related information.

To prevent **bind** from supplying an implicit object reference to the *callback*, specify your own object as the first element of the array:

> $a->**bind**(*eventDescriptor*, [$b => 'Delete']);

So **bind** calls **Delete** with widget $b instead of $a.

Common Widget Options

Some of the widget options common to several widgets are described here for brevity. For options that take screen units, values are in pixels unless an optional one letter suffix modifier is present — c (cm), i (inch), m (mm), or p (points).

`-activebackground` => *color*
> Background color of widget when it is active.

`-activeborderwidth` => *width*
> Width in screen units of widget border when it is active.

`-activeforeground` => *color*
> Foreground color of widget when it is active.

`-anchor` => *anchorPos*
> How information is positioned inside widget. Valid *anchorPos* values are n, ne, e, se, s, sw, w, nw, and center.

`-background` => *color*
> Background color of widget in normal state.

`-bitmap` => *bitmap*
> Bitmap to display in the widget (error, gray12, gray25, gray50, gray75, hourglass, info, questhead, question, warning, @*pathName*).

-borderwidth => *width*

Width in screen units of widget border in normal state.

-command => *callback*

A Perl/Tk callback describing the Perl code to run when widget is invoked.

-cursor => [*bitmap, mask, foreground, background*]

An array reference describing the cursor to display when mouse pointer is in widget.

-disabledforeground => *color*

Foreground color of widget when it is disabled.

-exportselection => *boolean*

Whether or not a selection in the widget should also be the X selection.

-font => *font*

Font to use when drawing text inside the widget.

-foreground => *color*

Foreground color of widget in normal state.

-highlightbackground => *color*

Color of the rectangle drawn around the widget when it does not have the input focus.

-highlightcolor => *color*

Color of the rectangle drawn around the widget when it has the input focus.

-highlightthickness => *width*

Width in screen units of highlight rectangle drawn around widget when it has the input focus.

-image => *image*

Image to display in the widget (see Images).

-insertbackground => *color*

Color to use as background in the area covered by the insertion cursor.

-insertborderwidth => *width*

Width in screen units of border to draw around the insertion cursor.

`-insertofftime =>` *milliseconds*
> Time the insertion cursor should remain "off" in each blink cycle.

`-insertontime =>` *milliseconds*
> Time the insertion cursor should remain "on" in each blink cycle.

`-insertwidth =>` *width*
> Width in screen units of the insertion cursor.

`-jump =>` *boolean*
> Whether to notify scrollbars and scales connected to the widget to delay updates until mouse button is released.

`-justify =>` left| center | right
> How multiple lines line up with each other.

`-orient =>` horizontal | vertical
> Which orientation widget should use in layout.

`-padx =>` *width*
> Extra external space in screen units to request for the widget in x-direction.

`-pady =>` *height*
> Extra external space in screen units to request for the widget in y-direction.

`-relief =>` flat |groove |raised |ridge |solid |sunken
> 3-D effect desired for the widget's border.

`-repeatdelay =>` *milliseconds*
> Time a button or key must be held down before it begins to auto-repeat.

`-repeatinterval =>` *milliseconds*
> Time between auto-repeats once action has begun.

`-selectbackground =>` *color*
> Background color to use when displaying selected items.

`-selectborderwidth =>` *width*
> Width in screen units of border to draw around selected items.

`-selectforeground => ` *color*

Foreground color to use when displaying selected items.

`-setgrid => ` *boolean*

Whether this widget controls the resizing grid for its toplevel window.

`-state => normal |disabled (|active ` for button-type widgets)

Current state of widget.

`-takefocus => ` *focusType*

If 0 or 1, signals that the widget should never or always take the focus. If *undef,* Tk decides. Otherwise, executes *focusType* as a *callback* with the widget reference as the first argument. Returned value must be 0, 1, or *undef.*

`-text => ` *string*

Text to be displayed inside the widget.

`-textvariable => ` *varRef*

A reference to a Perl scalar variable which contains a text string to be displayed inside the widget, or which is modified by the widget.

`-troughcolor => ` *color*

Color to use for the rectangular trough areas in widget.

`-underline => ` *index*

Integer index of a character to underline in the widget.

`-wraplength => ` *length*

Maximum line length in screen units for word-wrapping.

`-xscrollcommand => ` *callback*

Subroutine and arguments to communicate with horizontal scrollbars.

`-yscrollcommand => ` *callback*

Subroutine and arguments to communicate with vertical scrollbars.

2. Perl/Tk Special Variables

`$Tk::library`
> Directory containing library of Tk modules, widgets, and scripts.

`$Tk::patchLevel`
> Integer specifying current patch level for Tcl/Tk.

`$Tk::strictMotif`
> When non-zero, Tk tries to adhere to Motif look-and-feel as closely as possible.

`$Tk::version`
> Current version of Tcl/Tk that Perl/Tk is based on, in *major.minor* form.

`$Tk::VERSION`
> Current version of Perl/Tk.

3. Widget Scroll Commands

The Canvas, Listbox, and Text widgets support the following scrolling commands. The Entry widget supports the **xview** command and the **scan** command with the y coordinate dropped.

Refer to the section *Perl/Tk Widgets* and learn how the Perl/Tk widget Scrolled greatly simplifies managing scrollbars.

$widget->**scanMark**($x, y$);
> Records x and y as widget's current view anchor.

$widget->**scanDragto**($x, y$);
> Shifts the view by 10 times the difference between the coordinates x and y and the current view anchor coordinates.

$widget->**xview**;
> Returns a two-element list specifying the fraction of the horizontal span of the widget at the left and right edges of the window.

$widget->**xviewMoveto**(*fraction*);
> Adjusts the view in the window so that *fraction* of the total width of the widget is off-screen to the left.

$widget->**xviewScroll**(*number* => units | pages);
> Shifts the view by *number* one-tenth (unit) or nine-tenth (pages) the window's width in the horizontal direction.

$widget->**yview**;
> Returns a two-element list specifying the fraction of the vertical span of the widget at the top and bottom edges of the window.

$widget->**yviewMoveto**(*fraction*);
> Adjusts the view in the window so that *fraction* of the total height of the widget is off-screen to the top.

$widget->**yviewScroll**(*number* => units | pages);
> Shifts the view by *number* one-tenth (unit) or nine-tenth (pages) the window's height in the vertical direction.

The Text widget also supports the following:

$text->**yview**(?-pickplace,? *index*);
> Changes view of widget's window to make character at *index* visible. If -pickplace is specified, *index* will appear at the top of the window.

The Entry (**xview** only) and Listbox widget also support the following:

$listbox->**xview**(*index*);
> Adjusts view so that character position *index* is at left edge.

$listbox->**yview**(*index*);
> Adjusts view so that element at *index* is at top of window.

4. The Canvas Widget

Canvas Options

-background
-borderwidth
-cursor
-height
-highlightbackground
-highlightcolor
-highlightthickness
-insertbackground
-insertborderwidth
-insertofftime
-insertontime
-insertwidth
-relief
-selectbackground
-selectborderwidth
-selectforeground
-takefocus
-width
-xscrollcommand
-yscrollcommand

-closeenough => *float*

How close the mouse cursor must be to an item before it is considered to be "inside" the item.

-confine => *boolean*

Whether it is allowable to set the canvas's view outside the scroll region.

-scrollregion => [*corners*]

Array reference of four coordinates describing the left, top, right, and bottom of a rectangular scrolling region.

-xscrollincrement => *distance*

Specifies the increment for horizontal scrolling in screen units.

-yscrollincrement => *distance*

Specifies the increment for vertical scrolling in screen units.

Coordinate examples: 5 (pixel), 2.2i (inch), 4.1c (cm), 3m (mm), 21p (pts)

Larger y-coordinates refer to points lower on the screen; larger x-coordinates refer to points farther to the right.

Character positions: *charIndex*, end, insert, sel.first, sel.last, @*x,y*

Canvas Commands

$canvas->**addtag**(*tag, searchSpec* ?, *arg, arg* ...?);
> Adds *tag* to the list of tags associated with each item that satisfies *searchSpec*. See *Canvas Search Specifications* below.

$canvas->**bbox**(*tagOrId* ?, *tagOrId* ...?);
> Returns a list (*x1, y1, x2, y2*) giving an *approximate* bounding box for all the items named by the *tagOrId* arguments.

$canvas->**bind**(*tagOrId* ?, *sequence* => *callback*?);
> Associates *callback* to be invoked on events specified with *sequence* with the items given by *tagOrId*. Use the **CanvasBind** method to create a binding for the canvas as a whole.

$canvas->**canvasx**(*screenx* ?, *gridspacing*?);
> Returns the canvas x-coordinate that is displayed at screen x-coordinate *screenx,* possibly rounding to nearest multiple of *gridspacing* units.

$canvas->**canvasy**(*screeny* ?, *gridspacing*?);
> Returns the canvas x-coordinate that is displayed at screen y-coordinate *screeny,* possibly rounding to nearest multiple of *gridspacing* units.

$canvas->**coords**(*tagOrId* ?, *x0, y0* ...?);
> Queries or modifies the coordinates that define an item.

$canvas->**create***Type*(*x, y* ?, *x, y* ...? ?, *-option=>value* ...?);
> Creates a new item of type *Type* at specified coordinates and with list options. Currently *Type* may be: **Arc, Bitmap, Image, Line, Oval, Polygon, Rectangle, Text,** or **Window.**

$canvas->**dchars**(*tagOrId, first* ?, *last*?);
> For items given by *tagOrId,* deletes the characters in the range given by *first* and *last* (defaults to *first*), inclusive.

$canvas->**delete**(?*tagOrId* ...?);
> Deletes each of the items given by each *tagOrId.*

$ *canvas*->**dtag**(*tagOrId* ?, *tagToDelete*?);
> Removes tag *tagToDelete* from the taglist of items given by *tagOrId*.

$ *canvas*->**find**(*searchSpec* ?, *arg, arg* ... ?);
> Returns a list of the items that satisfy the specification *searchSpec*. See *Canvas Search Specifications* below.

$ *canvas*->**focus**(*tagOrId*);
> Sets the focus to the first textual item given by *tagOrId*.

$ *canvas*->**gettags**(*tagOrId*);
> Returns a list of the tags associated with the first item given by *tagOrId*.

$ *canvas*->**icursor**(*tagOrId, index*);
> Sets the insertion cursor for the item(s) given by *tagOrId* to just before the character position *index*.

$ *canvas*->**index**(*tagOrId, index*);
> Returns a decimal string giving the numerical index within *tagOrId* corresponding to character position *index*.

$ *canvas*->**insert**(*tagOrId, beforeThis, string*);
> Inserts *string* just before character position *beforeThis* in items given by *tagOrId* that support textual insertion.

$ *canvas*->**itemcget**(*tagOrId, -option*);
> Returns the value *-option* for the item given by *tagOrId*.

$ *canvas*->**itemconfigure**(*tagOrId* ?, *-option => value* ... ?);
> Modifies item-specific options for the items given by *tagOrId*.

$ *canvas*->**lower**(*tagOrId* ?, *belowThis*?);
> Moves the items given by *tagOrId* to a new position in the display list just before the first item given by *belowThis*.

$ *canvas*->**move**(*tagOrId, xAmount, yAmount*);
> Moves the items given by *tagOrId* in the canvas coordinate space by adding *xAmount* and *yAmount* to each item's *x* and *y* coordinates, respectively.

$canvas->**postscript**(*?-option => value …?*);
> Generates an Encapsulated Postscript representation for part or all of the canvas. See *Canvas Postscript Options* below.

$canvas->**raise**(*tagOrId ?, aboveThis?*);
> Moves the items given by *tagOrId* to a new position in the display list just after the first item given by *aboveThis*.

$canvas->**scale**(*tagOrId, xOrigin, yOrigin, xScale, yScale*);
> Rescales items given by *tagOrId* in canvas coordinate space to change the distance from *xOrigin, yOrigin* by a factor of *xScale, yScale*, respectively.

$canvas->**scan**(*args*);
> See *Widget Scroll Commands* above.

$canvas->**selectAdjust**(*tagOrId, index*);
> Adjusts nearest end of current selection in *tagOrId* to be at *index* and set the other end to be the new selection anchor.

$canvas->**selectClear**;
> Clears the selection if it is in the widget.

$canvas->**selectFrom**(*tagOrId, index*);
> Sets the selection anchor in *tagOrId* to just before the character at *index*.

$canvas->**selectItem**;
> Returns id of the selected item. Returns a empty string if there is none.

$canvas->**selectTo**(*tagOrId, index*);
> Sets the selection to extend between *index* and anchor point in *tagOrId*.

$canvas->**type**(*tagOrId*);
> Returns the type of the first item given by *tagOrId*.

$canvas->**xview| yview**(*args*);
> See *Widget Scroll Commands* above.

Canvas Search Specifications

above => *tagOrId*
> Selects the item just after the one given by *tagOrId* in the display list.

all
> Selects all the items in the canvas.

below => *tagOrId*
> Selects the item just before the one given by *tagOrId* in the display list.

closest => *x, y ?, halo? ?, start?*
> Selects the topmost, closest item to *@x,y* that is below *start* in the display list. Any item closer than *halo* to the point is considered to overlap it.

enclosed => *x1, y1, x2, y2*
> Selects all the items completely enclosed within *x1, y1, x2, y2.*

overlapping => *x1, y1, x2, y2*
> Selects all the items that overlap or are enclosed within *x1, y1, x2, y2.*

withtag => *tagOrId*
> Selects all the items given by *tagOrId.*

Canvas Item Types

$canvas->**createArc**(*x1, y1, x2, y2 ?, -option => value ... ?*);

```
-fill => color              -tags => tagList
-outline => color           -width => outlineWidth
-stipple => bitmap
```

```
-extent => degrees
```
> Size of the angular range occupied by arc.

```
-outlinestipple => bitmap
```
> Bitmap stipple to use to draw arc's outline.

`-start => `*degrees*
>   Starting angle measured from 3-o'clock position.

`-style => pieslice I chord I arc`
>   How to "complete" the region of the arc.

$canvas->**createBitmap**(*x, y* ?, *-option => value* ...?);

`-anchor => ` *anchorPos*	`-foreground => ` *color*
`-background => ` *color*	`-tags => ` *tagList*
`-bitmap => ` *bitmap*	

$canvas->**createImage**(*x, y* ?, *-option => value* ... ?);

`-anchor => ` *anchorPos*	`-tags => ` *tagList*
`-image => ` *image*	

$canvas->**createLine**(*x1, y1, ... xN, yN* ?, *-option => value* ...?);

`-fill => ` *color*	`-tags => ` *tagList*
`-smooth => ` *boolean*	`-width => ` *outlineWidth*
`-stipple => ` *bitmap*	

`-arrow => none I first I last I both`
>   Specify on which ends of the line to draw arrows.

`-arrowshape => ` *shape*
>   Three-element list which describes shape of arrow.

`-capstyle => butt I projecting I round`
>   How to draw caps at endpoints of the line. Default is
>   `butt`.

`-joinstyle => bevel I miter I round`
>   How joints are to be drawn at vertices. Default is `miter`.

`-splinesteps => ` *number*
>   Degree of smoothness desired for curves.

$canvas->**createOval**(*x1, y1, x2, y2* ?, *-option => value* ...?);

`-fill => ` *color*	`-tags => ` *tagList*
`-outline => ` *color*	`-width => ` *outlineWidth*
`-stipple => ` *bitmap*	

$canvas->**createPolygon**(*x1, y1, ... xN, yN ?, -option =>*
value ...?);

-fill => *color*	-stipple => *bitmap*
-outline => *color*	-tags => *tagList*
-smooth => *boolean*	-width => *outlineWidth*

-splinesteps => *number*
   Degree of smoothness desired for curved perimeter.

$canvas->**createRectangle**(*x1, y1, x2, y2 ?, -option => value*
...?);

-fill => *color*	-tags => *tagList*
-outline => *color*	-width => *outlineWidth*
-stipple => *bitmap*	

$canvas->**createText**(*x, y ?,-option => value ...?);*

-anchor => *anchorPos*	-stipple => *bitmap*
-fill => *color*	-tags => *taglist*
-font => *font*	-text => *string*

-justify => left | right | center
   How to justify text within its bounding region.

-width => *lineLength*
   Maximum line length for the text. If zero, break only on
   \n.

$canvas->**createWindow**(*x, y ?,-option => value ...?);*

-anchor => *anchorPos*	-tags => *tagList*
-height => *height*	Height in screen units to assign item's window.
-width => *width*	Width in screen units to assign item's window.
-window => *widgetRef*	Widget to associate with item.

Canvas PostScript Options

$canvas->**postscript**(*?-option => value ...?);*

-colormap => *varRef*

Specifies a color mapping to use where *varRef* is an array variable whose elements specify PostScript code to set a particular color value.

-colormode => color I grey I mono

Specifies how to output color information.

-file => *pathName*

Specifies the name of the file in which to write the Post-Script. If not specified, the PostScript is returned as the result of the command.

-fontmap => *varRef*

Specifies a font mapping to use where *varRef* is an array variable whose elements specify the PostScript font and size to use as a two-element list.

-height => *size*

Specifies the height of the area of the canvas to print. Defaults to the height of the canvas window.

-pageanchor => *anchor*

Specifies which point of the printed area should appear over the positioning point on the page. Defaults to center.

-pageheight => *size*

Specifies that the PostScript should be scaled in both x and y so that the printed area is *size* high on the PostScript page.

-pagewidth => *size*

Specifies that the PostScript should be scaled in both x and y so that the printed area is *size* wide on the Post-Script page.

-pagex => *position*

Sets the x-coordinate of the positioning point on the page to *position*.

-pagey => *position*
> Sets the y-coordinate of the positioning point on the page to *position*.

-rotate => *boolean*
> Whether the printed area is to be rotated 90 degrees (landscape).

-width => *size*
> Specifies the width of the area of the canvas to print. Defaults to the width of the canvas window.

-x => *position*
> Sets the x-coordinate of the left edge of canvas area to print.

-y => *position*
> Sets the y-coordinate of the top edge of canvas area to print.

5. *The Entry Widget*

Entry Widget Options

```
-background              -insertbackground
-borderwidth             -insertborderwidth
-cursor                  -insertofftime
-exportselection         -insertontime
-font                    -insertwidth
-foreground              -justify
-highlightbackground     -relief
-highlightcolor          -selectbackground
-highlightthickness      -selectborderwidth
-selectforeground        -textvariable
-state                   -width
-takefocus
```

-show *char*
> Disguises each visible character in the entry with *char*.

Entry Indices: *number*(starts at 0), anchor, end, insert, sel.first, sel.last, @*x*

Entry Widget Commands

$entry->**bbox**(*index*);
    Returns a list (*x, y, width, height*) giving an approximate
    bounding box of character given by *index*.

$entry->**delete**(*first ?, last?*);
    Deletes characters from *first* through character just before
    last.

$entry->**get**;
    Returns the $entry's string.

$entry->**icursor**(*index*);
    Displays insertion cursor just before character at *index*.

$entry->**index**(*index*);
    Returns the numerical index corresponding to *index*.

$entry->**insert**(*index, string*);
    Inserts *string* just before character at *index*.

$entry->**scan**(*-option, args*);
    See *Widget Scroll Commands* above.

$entry->**selectionAdjust**(*index*);
    Adjusts nearest end of current selection to be at *index* and
    sets the other end to the anchor point.

$entry->**selectionClear**;
    Clears the selection if currently in the widget.

$entry->**selectionFrom**(*index*);
    Sets the anchor point to be at *index*.

$entry->**selectionPresent**;
    Returns 1 if any characters are selected, 0 otherwise.

$entry->**selectionRange**(*start, end*);
    Selects the characters from *start* through character just
    before *end*.

$entry->**selectionTo**(*index*);
    Sets the selection to extend between *index* and anchor
    point.

6. The Listbox Widget

Listbox Widget Options

```
-background              -relief
-borderwidth             -selectbackground
-cursor                  -selectborderwidth
-exportselection         -selectforeground
-font                    -setgrid
-foreground              -takefocus
-height                  -width
-highlightbackground     -xscrollcommand
-highlightcolor          -yscrollcommand
-highlightthickness
```

`-selectmode  single|browse|multiple|extended`

Listbox Indices: *number* (starts at 0), `active`, `anchor`, `end`, @*x,y*

Listbox Widget Commands

$*listbox*->**activate**(*index*);
> Sets the active element to *index*.

$*listbox*->**bbox**(*index*);
> Returns a list (*x, y, width, height*) giving an *approximate* bounding box of character given by *index*.

$*listbox*->**curselection**;
> Returns list of indices of all elements currently selected.

$*listbox*->**delete**(*index1 ?, index2?*);
> Deletes range of elements from *index1* to *index2* (defaults to *index1*).

$*listbox*->**get**(*index1 ?, index2?*);
> Returns as a list contents of elements from *index1* to *index2*.

$*listbox*->**index**(*index*);
> Returns position *index* in *number* notation.

$ *listbox*->**insert**(*index* ?, *element* ...?);
    Inserts specified elements just before element at *index*.

$ *listbox*->**nearest**(*y*);
    Returns index of element nearest to *y*-coordinate.

$ *listbox*->**scan**(*args*);
    See *Widget Scroll Commands* above.

$ *listbox*->**selectionAnchor**(*index*);
    Sets the selection anchor to element at *index*.

$ *listbox*->**selectionClear**(*first* ?, *last*?);
    Deselects elements between *first* and *last* inclusive.

$ *listbox*->**selectionIncludes**(*index*);
    Returns 1 if element at *index* is selected, 0 otherwise.

$ *listbox*->**selectionSet**(*first* ?,*last*?);
    Adds all elements between *first* and *last* inclusive to selection.

$ *listbox*->**see**(*index*);
    Adjusts the view in window so element at *index* is completely visible.

$ *listbox*->**size**
    Returns number of elements in *listbox*.

$ *listbox*->**xview**| **yview**(*args*);
    See *Widget Scroll Commands* above.

7. *The Menu Widget*

Menu Widget Options

```
-activebackground        -cursor
-activeborderwidth       -disabledforeground
-activeforeground        -font
-background              -foreground
-borderwidth             -relief
```

-postcommand => *callback*

Specify *callback* to invoke immediately before the menu is posted.

-selectcolor => *color*

Specifies indicator color for checkbutton and radiobutton entries.

-tearoff => *boolean*

Whether to include a tear-off entry at top of menu.

-tearoffcommand => *callback*

Specifies command to be run when menu is torn off. The name of the menu and the new torn-off window will be appended on invocation.

-title => *string*

Uses *string* for window title when the menu is torn off.

-type => *type*

Used during creation to specify menubar, tearoff, or normal.

Entry Types: cascade, checkbutton, command, radiobutton, separator

Menu Indices: *number* (starts at 0, normally the *tearoff* item), active, last, none, @*y*, *matchPattern*

Menu Widget Commands

$ *menu*->**activate**(*index*);

Changes state of entry at *index* to be sole active entry in menu.

$ *menu*->**add**(*type* ?, -*option* => *value* ...?);

Adds new entry of type *type* to bottom of menu. See below for options.

$ *menu*->**cascade**(?-*option* => *value* ...?);

Adds new cascade entry to bottom of menu. See below for options.

$ *menu*->**checkbutton**(*?-option => value ...?*);
> Adds new checkbutton entry to bottom of menu. See below for options.

$ *menu*->**clone**(*newMenuName ?, cloneType?*);
> Clones $ *menu* as a new menu *newMenuName* of type *cloneType* (see -type).

$ *menu*->**command**(*?-option => value ...?*);
> Adds new command entry to bottom of menu. See below for options.

$ *menu*->**delete**(*index1 ?, index2?*);
> Deletes all entries between *index1* and *index2* inclusive.

$ *menu*->**entrycget**(*index, -option*);
> Returns current value of *-option* for entry at *index*.

$ *menu*->**entryconfigure**(*index ?, -option =>value ...?*);
> Sets option values for entry at *index*.

$ *menu*->**index**(*index*);
> Returns the numerical index corresponding to *index*.

$ *menu*->**insert**(*index, type ?, -option => value ...?*);
> Same as **add** but inserts new entry just before entry at *index*.

$ *menu*->**invoke**(*index*);
> Invokes the action of the menu entry at *index*.

$ *menu*->**post**(*x, y*);
> Displays menu on screen at root-window coordinates given by *x, y*.

$ *menu*->**postcascade**(*index*);
> Posts submenu associated with cascade entry at *index*.

$ *menu*->**radiobutton**(*?-option => value ...?*);
> Adds new radiobutton entry to bottom of menu. See below for options.

$menu->**separator**(*?-option* => *value* ...?);

Adds new separator entry to bottom of menu. See below for options.

$menu->**type**(*index*);

Returns type of menu entry at *index*.

$menu->**unpost**;

Unmaps window so it is no longer displayed.

$menu->**ypostion**(*index*);

Returns the y-coordinate within the menu window of the topmost pixel in the entry specified by *index*.

Menu Entry Options

The following options work for all cascade, checkbutton, command, and radiobutton entries unless otherwise specified.

```
-activebackground        -foreground
-activeforeground        -image
-background              -state
-bitmap                  -underline
-font
```

-accelerator => *string*

Specifies string to display at right side of menu entry.

-columnbreak => *value*

When *value* is 1, entry appears at top of a new column in menu.

-command => *callback*

callback to execute when the entry is invoked.

-hidemargin => *value*

When *value* is 1, the standard margins are not drawn around entry.

-indicatoron => *boolean*

Whether indicator for checkbutton or radiobutton entry should be displayed.

-label => *string*
    Textual string to display on left side of menu entry.

-menu => *menuRef*
    menuRef of a menu to post when cascade entry is active.

-offvalue => *value*
    Value to store in checkbutton entry's associated variable
    when deselected.

-onvalue => *value*
    Value to store in checkbutton entry's associated variable
    when selected.

-selectcolor => *color*
    Color for indicator in checkbutton and radiobutton
    entries.

-selectimage => *image*
    Image to draw in indicator for checkbutton and radio-
    button entries.

-value => *value*
    Value to store in radiobutton entry's associated variable
    when selected.

-variable => *varRef*
    Name of global variable to set when checkbutton or
    radiobutton is selected.

8. *The Text Widget*

Text Widget Options

-background	-insertwidth
-borderwidth	-padx
-cursor	-pady
-exportselection	-relief
-font	-selectbackground
-foreground	-selectborderwidth
-height	-selectforeground
-highlightbackground	-setgrid
-highlightcolor	-state

```
-highlightthickness          -takefocus
-insertbackground            -width
-insertborderwidth           -xscrollcommand
-insertofftime               -yscrollcommand
-insertontime
```

-spacing1 => *size*   Space in screen units above
                       paragraphs.

-spacing2 => *size*   Space in screen units between
                       paragraph lines.

-spacing3 => *size*   Space in screen units below
                       paragraphs.

-tabs => *tabList*
  Set of tab stops as a list of screen distances giving their
  positions. Each stop may be followed by one of left,
  right, center, or numeric.

-wrap => none | char | word
  How to wrap lines.

Text Indices

Syntax: *base ?modifier ... ?*

Base: *line.char* (*line* starts at 1, *char* starts at 0), @*x,y*,
            end, *mark*, *tag*.first, *tag*.last, *widgetRef*
            (embedded window), *image* (embedded image)

Modifier: *count* chars, *count* lines, linestart,
            lineend, wordstart, wordend

Ranges: Ranges include all characters from the start index
            up to but not including the character at the stop
            index.

Text Tag Options

```
-background          -relief
-borderwidth         -spacing1
-font                -spacing2
```

`-foreground` `-justify`	`-spacing3` `-wrap`
`-bgstipple => `*bitmap*	Stipple pattern for background.
`-fgstipple => `*bitmap*	Stipple pattern for foreground.
`-lmargin1 => `*size*	Left margin of first line.
`-lmargin2 => `*size*	Left margin of wrapped lines.
`-offset => `*size*	Offset of baseline from normal baseline.
`-overstrike => `*boolean*	Whether to overstrike text.
`-rmargin => `*size*	Right margin of all lines.
`-tabs => `*tabList*	Set of tab stops (see `-tabs` above).
`-underline => `*boolean*	Whether to underline text.

Text Embedded Window Options

Use *-window* to pass a Perl/Tk widget reference to **windowCreate**. Manage embedded windows with **windowConfigure** and **windowCget**.

`-align => top | center | bottom | baseline`
 Where window is displayed on the line.

`-create => `*callback*
 Subroutine to create and return a widget reference if no `-window` option is given.

`-padx => `*width*
 Extra space in screen units to leave on the left and right of the window.

`-pady => `*height*
 Extra space in screen units to leave on the top and bottom of the window.

`-stretch => `*boolean*
 Whether window should be stretched vertically to fill line.

-window => *widgetRef*
　　Widget to display.

Text Embedded Image Options

-align => top | center | bottom | baseline
　　Where image is displayed on the line.

-image => *image*
　　Specifies Tk image to use for embedded image.

-name => *imageName*
　　Specifies name which may be used to reference the
　　embedded image.

-padx => *width*
　　Extra space in screen units to leave on the left and right
　　side of image.

-pady => *height*
　　Extra space in screen units to leave on the top and bottom
　　of image.

Text Widget Commands

$*text*->**bbox**(*index*);
　　Returns a list (*x, y, width, height*) giving an approximate
　　bounding box of character given by *index*.

$*text*->**compare**(*index1, op, index2*);
　　Compares indices *index1* and *index2* according to rela-
　　tional operater *op*.

$*text*->**delete**(*index1 ?, index2?*);
　　Deletes range of characters (*index2* defaults to *index1* +
　　1 *char*).

$*text*->**dlineinfo**(*index*);
　　Returns a list (*x, y, width, height, baseline*) describing the
　　screen area taken by display line at *index*.

$text->**dump**(*?switches, ? index1 ?, index2?*);
> Returns detailed info on text widget contents in range
> *index1* to *index2*. Switches include -all, -mark, -tag,
> -text, -window for specifying type of info returned. The
> switch -command => *callback* exists to invoke a proce-
> dure on each element type in the range.

$text->**get**(*index1 ?, index2?*);
> Returns string of characters in range (*index2* defaults to
> *index1* + 1 *char*).

$text->**imageCget**(*index, option*);
> Returns current value of *option* for embedded image at
> *index*.

$text->**imageConfigure**(*index ?, option => ?value??*);
> Modifies embedded image-specific options for the image
> at *index*.

$text->**imageCreate**(*index ?, option => value?*);
> Creates a new embedded image at position *index* with
> specified options.

$text->**imageNames**;
> Returns list of names of all images embedded in text
> widget.

$text->**index**(*index*);
> Returns position *index* in *line.char* notation.

$text->**insert**(*index ?, string ?, tagList, string, tagList …??*);
> Inserts *string* into text at *index* applying tags from *tagList*.

$text->**markGravity**(*markName* => ?left | right?);
> Returns (or sets) which adjacent character a mark is
> attached to.

$text->**markNames**
> Returns a list of the names of all marks currently set.

$text->**markNext** | **markPrevious**(*index*);
> Returns name of next/previous mark at or after/before
> *index*.

$ *text*->**markSet**(*markName* => *index*);
> Sets mark *markName* to position just before character at *index*.

$ *text*->**markUnset**(*markName* ?, *markName* …?);
> Removes each mark specified so they are no longer usuable as indices.

$ *text*->**scan**(*args*);
> See *Widget Scroll Commands* above.

$ *text*->**search**(?*switches*, ? *pattern*, *index* ?, *stopIndex*?);
> Returns index of first character matching *pattern* in text range *index* to *stopIndex*. Switches: `-forwards`, `-backwards`, `-exact`, `-regexp`, `-count` => *var*, `-nocase`}

$ *text*->**see**(*index*);
> Adjusts the view in window so character at *index* is completely visible.

$ *text*->**tagAdd**(*tagName*, *index1* ?, *index2*?);
> Applies tag *tagName* to range (*index2* defaults to *index1* + 1 char).

$ *text*->**tagBind**(*tagName* ?, *sequence* ?, *script*??);
> Arranges for *script* to be run whenever event *sequence* occurs for a character with tag *tagName*.

$ *text*->**tagCget**(*tagName* => *-option*);
> Returns current value of *-option* for tag *tagName*.

$ *text*->**tagConfigure**(*tagName* ?, *-option* ?, *value* ?, *-option* => *value* …?);
> Modifies tag-specific options for the tag *tagName*.

$ *text*->**tagDelete**(*tagName* ?, *tagName* …?);
> Deletes all tag information for given tags.

$ *text*->**tagLower**(*tagName* ?, *belowThis*?);
> Changes priority of tag *tagName* so it is just below tag *belowThis*.

$text->**tagNames**(*?index?*);

Returns a list of the names of all tags associated with character at *index*. If *index* is not given, returns list of all tags defined in widget.

$text->**tagNextrange**(*tagName, index1 ?, index2?*);

Searches character range *index1* to *index2* (default end) for the first region tagged with *tagName*. Returns character range of region found.

$text->**tagPrevrange**(*tagName, index1 ?, index2?*);

Like **tagNextrange** but searches backwards from *index1* to *index2* (default 1.0).

$text->**tagRaise**(*tagName ?, aboveThis?*);

Changes priority of tag *tagName* so it is just above tag *aboveThis*.

$text->**tagRanges**(*tagName*);

Returns a list describing all character ranges tagged with *tagName*.

$text->**tagRemove**(*tagName, index1 ?, index2?*);

Removes tag *tagName* for all characters in range *index1* to *index2*.

$text->**windowCget**(*index, -option*);

Returns current value of *-option* for embedded window at *index*.

$text->**windowConfigure**(*index ?, -option ? => value …?*);

Modifies embedded window-specific options for the window at *index*.

$text->**windowCreate**(*index ?, -option => value …?*);

Creates a new embedded window at position *index* with specified options.

$text->**windowNames**;

Returns list of names of all windows embedded in widget.

$text->**xview| yview**(*args*);

See *Widget Scroll Commands* above.

9. Other Standard Widgets

Button

-activebackground
-activeforeground
-anchor
-background
-bitmap
-borderwidth
-command
-cursor
-disabledforeground
-font
-foreground
-height
-highlightbackground
-highlightcolor

-highlightthickness
-image
-justify
-padx
-pady
-relief
-state
-takefocus
-text
-textvariable
-underline
-width
-wraplength

-default=>*state*
   Set state of default string, one of active, normal, or
   disabled.

$*button*->**flash**;
   Alternate checkbutton between active and normal colors.

$*button*->**invoke**;
   Toggle the selection state of the button and invoke the
   callback specified with -command.

Checkbutton

-activebackground
-activeforeground
-anchor
-background
-bitmap
-borderwidth
-command
-cursor
-disabledforeground
-font

-highlightthickness
-image
-justify
-padx
-pady
-relief
-state
-takefocus
-text
-textvariable

```
-foreground                    -underline
-height                        -width
-highlightbackground           -wraplength
-highlightcolor
```

-indicatoron => *boolean*
   Whether or not the indicator should be drawn.

-offvalue => *value*
   Value given to variable specified with -variable option
   when the checkbutton is deselected.

-onvalue => *value*
   Value given to variable specified with -variable option
   when the checkbutton is selected.

-selectcolor => *color*
   Color used to fill in indicator when selected.

-selectimage => *image*
   Image displayed in indicator when selected.

-variable => *varRef*
   Variable to associate with checkbutton.

$*checkbutton*->**deselect**;
   Deselect the checkbutton.

$*checkbutton*->**flash**;
   Alternates checkbutton between active and normal colors.

$*checkbutton*->**invoke**;
   Toggles the selection state of the checkbutton and
   invokes the *callback* specified with -command, if any.

$*checkbutton*->**select**;
   Selects the checkbutton.

$*checkbutton*->**toggle**;
   Toggles the selection state of the checkbutton.

Frame

```
-borderwidth                   -highlightthickness
-cursor                        -relief
```

```
-height                      -takefocus
-highlightbackground         -width
-highlightcolor
```

-background => *color*

Same as standard except it may be the empty string to pre-serve colormap.

-class => *name*

Class name to use in querying the option database and for bindings.

-colormap => *colormap*

Colormap to use for the window if different from parent.

-container => *boolean*

Whether the frame will be a container to embed another application.

-visual => *visual*

Visual info to use for the window if different from parent.

Label

```
-anchor                      -bitmap
-background                  -borderwidth
-cursor                      -padx
-font                        -pady
-foreground                  -relief
-height                      -takefocus
-highlightbackground         -text
-highlightcolor              -textvariable
-highlightthickness          -underline
-image                       -width
-justify                     -wraplength
```

Menubutton

```
-activebackground            -highlightthickness
-activeforeground            -image
-anchor                      -justify
-background                  -padx
-bitmap                      -pady
```

-borderwidth	-relief
-cursor	-state
-disabledforeground	-takefocus
-font	-text
-foreground	-textvariable
-height	-underline
-highlightbackground	-width
-highlightcolor	-wraplength

-direction => *direction*

>   Where to pop up menu; *direction* is one of above, below,
>   left, right, or flush.

-indicatoron => *boolean*

>   If true, then a small indicator will be displayed on the but-
>   ton's right side and the default menu bindings will treat
>   this as an option menubutton.

-menu => *menuRef*

>   Menu widget to post when button is invoked.

-menuitems => [[*type, label* ?, *-option* => *value*?]]

>   A list of menuitem *types*, like **button**, with the text *label*
>   and optional parameters. -menuitems can be nested.
>   This allows you to create a menubutton's entire menu
>   with a data structure. (See *The Menu Widget*.)

Message

-anchor	-justify
-background	-padx
-borderwidth	-pady
-cursor	-relief
-font	-takefocus
-foreground	-text
-highlightbackground	-textvariable
-highlightcolor	-width
-highlightthickness	

-aspect => *integer*

>   Displays text according to the ratio of text width to text
>   height times 100.

Radiobutton

-activebackground	-highlightthickness
-activeforeground	-image
-anchor	-justify
-background	-padx
-bitmap	-pady
-borderwidth	-relief
-command	-state
-cursor	-takefocus
-disabledforeground	-text
-font	-textvariable
-foreground	-underline
-height	-width
-highlightbackground	-wraplength
-highlightcolor	

-indicatoron => *boolean*
> Whether or not the indicator should be drawn.

-selectcolor => *color*
> Color used to fill in indicator when selected.

-selectimage => *image*
> Image displayed in indicator when selected.

-value => *value*
> Value given to variable specified with -variable option when the radiobutton is selected.

-variable => *varRef*
> Variable to associate with radiobutton.

$radiobutton->**deselect**;
> Deselects the radiobutton.

$radiobutton->**flash**;
> Alternates radiobutton between active and normal colors.

$radiobutton->**invoke**;
> Toggles the selection state of the radiobutton and invokes the *callback* specified with -command, if any.

$ *radiobutton*->**select**;
    Selects the radiobutton.

Scale

-activebackground	-highlightthickness
-background	-orient
-borderwidth	-relief
-cursor	-repeatdelay
-foreground	-repeatinterval
-font	-state
-highlightbackground	-takefocus
-highlightcolor	-troughcolor

-bigincrement => *float*
    A real value to use for large increments of the scale.

-command => *callback*
    Specifies a *callback* to invoke when scale's value is
    changed. The scale's value will be appended as an addi-
    tional argument.

-digits => *integer*
    An integer specifying how many significant digits should
    be retained.

-from => *number*
    A real value corresponding to the left or top end of the
    scale.

-label => *string*
    A string to display as label for the scale.

-length => *size*
    Specifies the height (width) for vertical (horizontal)
    scales.

-resolution => *number*
    Rounds the scale's value to an even multiple of the real
    value, *number.*

-showvalue => *boolean*
    Whether or not scale's current value should be displayed
    in side label.

`-sliderlength => ` *size*

    Size of the slider, measured along the slider's long dimension.

`-sliderrelief => ` *relief*

    Specifies the relief used to display the slider.

`-tickinterval => ` *number*

    A real value to specify the spacing between numerical tick marks displayed.

`-to => ` *number*

    A real value corresponding to the right or bottom end of the scale.

`-variable => ` *varRef*

    Name of a global variable to link to the scale.

`-width => ` *width*

    Narrow dimension of scale (not including border).

$scale->**coords**(*?value?*);

    Returns x and y coordinates of point correspoinding to *value*.

$scale->**get**(*?x, y?*);

    If *x, y* is given, returns scale value at that coordiante postion. Otherwise, scale's current value is returned.

$scale->**identify**(*x, y*);

    Returns string indicating part of scale at postion *x, y*. May be one of `slider`, `trough1`, `trough2`, or empty.

$scale->**set**(*value*);

    Changes the current value of scale to *value*.

Scrollbar

`-activebackground`	`-jump`
`-background`	`-orient`
`-borderwidth`	`-relief`
`-cursor`	`-repeatdelay`
`-highlightbackground`	`-repeatinterval`

```
-highlightcolor          -takefocus
-highlightthickness      -troughcolor
```

`-activerelief => ` *relief*

Relief to use when displaying the element that is active.

`-command => ` *callback*

Specifies *callback* to invoke for changing the view in the widget associated with the scrollbar.

`-elementborderwidth => ` *width*

Width of borders around internal elements (arrows and slider).

`-width => ` *width*

Narrow dimension of scrollbar (not including border).

Elements: arrow1, trough1, slider, trough2, arrow2

$ *scrollbar*->**activate**(*?element?*);

Display *element* with active attributes.

$ *scrollbar*->**delta**(*deltaX, deltaY*);

Returns fractional position change for slider movement of *deltaX, deltaY*.

$ *scrollbar*->**fraction**(*x, y*);

Returns a real number between 0 and 1 indicating where the point given by pixel coords *x, y* lies in the trough area of the scrollbar.

$ *scrollbar*->**get**;

Returns current scrollbar settings as the list (*first, last*).

$ *scrollbar*->**identify**(*x, y*);

Returns name of element under pixel coords *x, y.*

$ *scrollbar*->**set**(*first, last*);

Describes current view of associated widget where *first* and *last* are the percentage distance from widget's beginning of the start and end of the view.

Toplevel

```
-borderwidth            -highlightthickness
-cursor                 -relief
-height                 -takefocus
-highlightbackground    -width
-highlightcolor
```

-background => *color*

    Same as standard, but may be empty to preserve color-map space.

-class => *string*

    Class name for the window to be used by option database.

-colormap => *colormap*

    Color map to use for window. May be the word new, widget reference of other toplevel, or empty for the default colormap of screen.

-container => *boolean*

    Whether toplevel is a container used to embed another application.

-menu => *menuref*

    Specifies the Toplevel's menu widget.

-screen => *screen*

    Screen on which to place the window.

-use => *windowID*

    Toplevel should be embedded inside window identified by *windowID* (see the Window Information command **id**) which was created as a container.

-visual => *visual*

    Specifies visual to use for window.

10. Perl/Tk Widgets

Here are Tix and other widgets particular to Perl/Tk. These widgets and their methods are defined via a **use** statement; for example:

---

use Tk::widgets qw/Tk::Adjuster Tk::ColorEditor/;

Adjuster

Adjuster allows size of packed widgets to be adjusted by the user.

```
-borderwidth              -highlightthickness
-cursor                   -relief
-height                   -takefocus
-highlightbackground      -width
-highlightcolor
```

$widget->**packAdjust**(?*packOptions*?);

> If $widget is packed with `-side => left|right` then width is adjusted. If packed `-side => top|bottom` then height is adjusted.

Balloon

Balloon provides the framework to create and attach help balloons to various widgets so that when the mouse pauses over the widget for more than a specified amount of time, a help balloon is popped up.

```
-borderwidth              -highlightbackground
-cursor                   -highlightcolor
-height                   -highlightthickness
-relief                   -width
-takefocus
```

`-initwait =>` *delay*

> Milliseconds to wait without activity before popping up a help balloon (default 350 milliseconds). This applies only to the popped up balloon; the status bar message is shown instantly.

`-state => balloon|status|both|none`

> Indicates that the help balloon, status bar help, both or none, respectively, should be activated when the mouse pauses over the client widget.

`-statusbar` => $widget
> Specifies the widget used to display the status message. This widget should accept the `-text` option and is typically a Label.

$*balloon*->**attach**($widget, -option => value ?,...?);
> Attaches the widget indicated by $*widget* to the help system.

`-statusmsg` => *statusMessage*
> The message shown on the status bar when the mouse passes over this client. If not specified but *-msg* is specified then the message displayed on the status bar is the same as the argument for *-msg*.

`-balloonmsg` => *balloonMessage*
> The message displayed in the balloon when the mouse pauses over the client. As with *-statusmsg,* if this is not specified, it takes its value from the *-msg* specification. If neither *-balloonmsg* nor *-msg* are specified, an empty balloon will pop up.

`-msg` => *defaultMessage*
> The catch-all for *-statusmsg* and *-balloonmsg.* This is a convenient way of specifying the same message to be displayed in both the balloon and the status bar for the client.

$*balloon*->**detach**($*widget*);
> Detaches the specified widget from the help system.

BrowseEntry

BrowseEntry is an enhanced version of LabEntry that provides a button to popup the choices of the possible values that the Entry may take.

`-borderwidth`	`-highlightthickness`
`-cursor`	`-relief`
`-height`	`-takefocus`
`-highlightbackground`	`-width`
`-highlightcolor`	

- `-listwidth => ` *width*

  Specifies the character width of the popup listbox.

- `-variable => ` *varRef*

  Where entered value is stored.

- `-browsecmd => ` *callback*

  Specifies a function to call when a selection is made. It is passed the widget and the text of the entry selected. This function is called after *varRef* has been assigned the value.

- `-listcmd => ` *callback*

  Specifies the function to call when the button next to the entry is pressed to popup the choices in the listbox. This is called before popping up the listbox, so it can be used to populate the entries in the listbox.

$browse->**insert**(*index, string*);

  Inserts the text of *string* at the specified *index*. This *string* then becomes available as one of the choices.

$browse->**delete**(*index1 ?, index2?*);

  Deletes items from *index1* to *index2*.

ColorEditor

ColorEditor is a general-purpose color selection widget that operates in RGB, HSB, or CMY color space.

`-borderwidth`	`-height`
`-cursor`	`-highlightbackground`
`-highlightcolor`	`-takefocus`
`-highlightthickness`	`-width`
`-relief`	

- `-title => ` *string*

  Toplevel title, default = ' '.

- `-cursor=> ` *cursor*

  A valid Tk cursor specification (default is *top_left_arrow*). This cursor is used over all ColorEditor hot spots.

- `-command => ` *callback*

  Optional replacement for **set_colors** color configurator.

`-widgets => [`*widgetList*`]`
    A reference to a list of widgets for the color configurator to color.

`-display_status => ` *boolean*
    True to display the ColorEditor status window when applying colors.

`-add_menu_item => ` *itemString*
    'SEP' (a separator), or a color attribute menu item.

`-delete_menu_item => ` *itemString*
    'SEP', a color attribute menu item, or color attribute menu ordinal.

$cedit->**Show**;
    Maps the ColorEditor toplevel window.

$cedit->**delete_widgets**([*widgetList*]);
    A reference to a list of widgets to remove from Color-Editor's consideration.

Dialog

Dialog creates a modal dialog window with a message and buttons and waits for a user response.

`-borderwidth`	`-highlightbackground`
`-cursor`	`-highlightcolor`
`-height`	`-highlightthickness`
`-relief`	`-width`
`-takefocus`	

`-title => ` *string*
    Title to display in the dialog's decorative frame.

`-text => ` *string*
    Message to display in the dialog widget.

`-bitmap => ` *bitmap*
    Bitmap to display in the dialog.

`-default_button => ` *string*
    Text label of the button that is to display the default string.

`-buttons => [@button_labels]`
> A reference to a list of button label strings.

$ *dialog*->**Show**(*?-global?*);
> Shows dialog and returns the selection as a string. The grab is local unless *-global* is specified.

DialogBox

Dialog creates a modal dialog window with a message and buttons and waits for a user response. Additionally it allows any widget in the top frame.

```
-borderwidth            -highlightthickness
-cursor                 -relief
-height                 -takefocus
-highlightbackground    -width
-highlightcolor
```

`-title => string`
> Title to display in the dialog's decorative frame.

`-text => string`
> Message to display in the dialog widget.

`-bitmap => bitmap`
> Bitmap to display in the dialog.

`-default_button => string`
> Text label of the button that is to display the default string.

`-buttons => [@button_labels]`
> A reference to a list of button label strings.

$ *dialog*->**add**(*widgetClass, ?options?*);
> Creates a widget of class *widgetClass* and add it to the dialogbox. Return the widget reference and **Advertise** it with the name *widgetClass*.

$ *dialog*->**Show**(*?-global?*);
> Shows dialog and return the selection as a string. The grab is local unless *-global* is specified.

DirTree

DirTree displays a list view of a directory, its previous directories and its sub-directories. A DirTree widget is derived from the Tree class and inherits all its commands, options, and subwidgets.

-background	-relief
-borderwidth	-selectbackground
-cursor	-selectborderwidth
-exportselection	-selectforeground
-font	-setGrid
-foreground	-takefocus
-height	-width
-highlightbackground	-xscrollcommand
-highlightcolor	-yscrollcommand
-highlightthickness	

-browsecmd => *callback*

Invoke the *callback* with the selected entry when it's browsed.

-command => *callback*

Invoke the *callback* with the selected entry when it's activated.

-dircmd => *callback*

Invoke the *callback* when a directory listing is needed for a particular directory. The first argument is the directory name, the second a *boolean* indicating whether hidden sub-directories should be listed.

-showhidden => *boolean*

Specifies whether hidden directories should be shown. Default is false.

-directory => *dirName*

The name of the current directory displayed in the widget.

$ *dtree*->**chdir**(*directory*);

Changes the current directory to *directory*.

ErrorDialog

A bizarre widget that intercepts error messages destined for
STDERR and instead displays them in a window. This widget
is magically created when the first background error occurs;
you just need to include a **use Tk::ErrorDialog** statement in
your program. To specify -cleanupcode or -appendtrace-
back manually instantiate the ErrorDialog object. (See
Tk::Error.)

```
-borderwidth                    -highlightthickness
-cursor                         -relief
-height                         -takefocus
-highlightbackground            -width
-highlightcolor
```

-cleanupcode => *callback*
  If special post-background error processing is required.

-appendtraceback => *boolean*
  Whether or not to append successive traceback messages.
  The default is true.

FileSelect

FileSelect is a widget for choosing files and/or directories.

```
-borderwidth                    -highlightbackground
-cursor                         -highlightcolor
-height                         -highlightthickness
-relief                         -width
-takefocus
```

-width => *width*
  Width of file and directory listboxes.

-height => *height*
  Height of file and directory listboxes.

-directory => *pathName*
  Starting directory pathname.

-filelabel => *string*
  Label for file Entry widget.

-filelistlabel => *string*
    Label for file Listbox widget.

-filter => *string*
    Limits search to the wildcard *string*.

-dirlabel => *string*
    Label for directory Entry widget.

-dirlistlabel => *string*
    Label for directory Listbox widget.

-accept => *callback*
    Overrides FileSelect; accept subroutine with your own.

-create => *boolean*
    True if it's okay to create directories.

-verify => [-verifyOptions]
    A list of Perl file test operators and/or *callbacks* to your
    own verify subroutine. The subroutine is implicitly called
    with a directory pathname and a file (or directory) name,
    and possibly optional arguments.

$*fsel*->**Show**;
    Map the FileSelect toplevel window; return selection or
    undef.

HList

HList is used to display any data that have a hierarchical
structure, for example, file system directory trees. The list
entries are indented and connected by branch lines according to their places in the hierachy.

-background	-relief
-borderwidth	-selectbackground
-cursor	-selectborderwidth
-exportselection	-selectforeground
-font	-setGrid
-foreground	-takefocus
-height	-width
-highlightbackground	-xscrollcommand

`-highlightcolor`   `-yscrollcommand`
`-highlightthickness`

`-browsecmd` => *callback*
> Specifies the callback invoked when the user browses through the entries in the HList widget.

`-columns` => *integer*
> Specifies the number of columns in this HList widget.

`-command` => *callback*
> Specifies the *callback* invoked when the user selects a list entry.

`-drawbranch` => *boolean*
> True if a branch line should be drawn to connect list entries to their parents.

`-header` => *boolean*
> Specifies whether headers should be displayed. (See the **header** method below.)

`-height` => *integer*
> Specifies the desired height for the window in number of characters.

`-indent` => pixels| textchars
> Specifies the amount of horizontal indentation between a list entry and its children.

`-indicator` => *boolean*
> Specifies whether the indicators should be displayed. (See the **indicator** methods below.)

`-indicatorcmd` => *callback*
> Specifies the *callback* executed when the user manipulates the indicator of an HList entry. The default callback is invoked with one implicit argument, the *entryPath* of the entry whose indicator has been triggered.

`-itemtype` => imagetext| text| window
> Specifies the type of display item.

-selectbackground => *color*
  Specifies the background color for the selected list entries.

-selectborderwidth => *width*
  Specifies the width of the 3-D border to draw around selected items.

-selectforeground => *color*
  Specifies the foreground color for the selected list entries.

-selectmode => single|browse|multiple|extended
  Specifies one of several styles for manipulating the selection.

-sizecmd => *callback*
  Specifies the *callback* executed whenever the HList widget changes size.

-separator => *string*
  Specifies the character to used as the separator character when intepreting the path-names of list entries. By default the character "." is used.

-width => *width*
  Specifies the desired width for the window in characters.

$*hlist*->**add**(*entryPath* ?, -option => *value*?);
  Creates a new list entry with the pathname *entryPath*. -*option* may be:

  -at => *index*
    Insert the new list at the position given by position *index*.

  -after => *index*
    Insert the new list entry after the entry identified by *index*.

  -before => *index*
    Insert the new list entry before the entry identified by *index*.

-data => *string*
  Specifies a Perl scalar to associate with this list entry.

`-itemtype => imagetext|text|window`
Specifies the type of display item.

`-state => normal|disabled`
Specifies whether this entry can be selected or invoked by the user.

$ *hlist*->**addchild**(*parent ?, -option => value?*);
Adds a new child entry to the children list of the list entry *parentPath* and returns the new *entryPath*.

$ *hlist*->**anchorSet**(*entryPath*);
Sets the anchor to the list entry identified by *entryPath*.

$ *hlist*->**anchorClear**;
Removes the anchor, if any.

$ *hlist*->**columnWidth**(*col ?, -char? ?, width?*);
Queries or sets the width of the column *col*.

$ *hlist*->**columnWidth**(*col =>* ' ');
An empty string indicates that the width of the column should be just wide enough to display the widest element in this column.

$ *hlist*->**columnWidth**(*col, width*);
Set column *col* to pixel width *width*.

$ *hlist*->**columnWidth**(*col, -char => nchars*);
The width is set to be the average width occupied by *nchars* number of characters of the font specified by the -font option.

$ *hlist*->**deleteAll**;
Deletes all list entries.

$ *hlist*->**deleteEntry**(*entryPath*);
Deletes list entry *entryPath*.

$ *hlist*->**deleteOffsprings**(*entryPath*);
Deletes all offsprings of *entryPath*.

$ *hlist*->**deleteSiblings**(*entryPath*);
Deletes all the list entries that share the parent *entryPath*.

$ *hlist*->**dragsiteSet**(*entryPath*);
> Sets the dragsite to the list entry identified by *entryPath*.

$ *hlist*->**dragsiteClear**;
> Removes the dragsite, if any.

$ *hlist*->**dropsiteSet**(*entryPath*);
> Sets the dropsite to the list entry identified by *entryPath*.

$ *hlist*->**dropsiteClear**;
> Removes the dropsite, if any.

$ *hlist*->**entrycget**(*entryPath, -option*);
> Returns the current value of the configuration option
> *-option* for *entryPath*.

$ *hlist*->**entryconfigure**(*entryPath ?, -option => value?*);
> Queries or modifies the configuration options of the list
> entry *entryPath*.

$ *hlist*->**headerCget**(*col, -option*);
> If column *col* has a header display item, returns the value
> of the specified option of the header item.

$ *hlist*->**headerConfigure**(*col ?, -option? ?=> value?*);
> Queries or modifies the configuration options of the
> header display item of column *col*.

$ *hlist*->**headerCreate**(*col ?, -itemtype => type? ?, -option =>*
> value ...?);
> Creates a new display item as the header for column *col*.

> `-borderwidth` => *width*
>> Specifies the border width of this header item.

> `-headerbackground` => *color*
>> Specifies the background color of this header item.

> `-relief` => *relief*
>> Specifies the relief type of the border of this header
>> item.

$ *hlist*->**headerDelete**(*col*);
> Deletes the header display item for column *col*.

$ *hlist*->**headerExists**(*col*);
>   Returns true if a header display item exists for column *col.*

$ *hlist*->**headerSize**(*col*);
>   Returns a two element list of the form [*width, height*] of
>   the header display item for column *col;*

$ *hlist*->**hideEntry**(*entryPath*);
>   Hides the list entry identified by *entryPath.*

$ *hlist*->**indicatorCget**(*entryPath, option*);
>   Returns the value of the specified option of the indicator
>   for *entryPath.*

$ *hlist*->**indicatorConfigure**(*entryPath ?, option? ?=> value?*);
>   Queries or modifies the configuration options of the indi-
>   cator display item of *entryPath.*

$ *hlist*->**indicatorCreate**(*entryPath ?, -itemtype => type? ?,
>   option => value*);
>   Creates a new display item as the indicator for *entryPath.*

$ *hlist*->**indicatorDelete**(*entryPath*);
>   Deletes the indicator display item for *entryPath.*

$ *hlist*->**indicatorExists**(*entryPath*);
>   Returns true if an indicator display item exists for *entry-
>   Path.*

$ *hlist*->**indicatorSize**(*entryPath*);
>   Returns a two-element list of the form [*width, height*] of
>   the indicator display item for *entryPath.*

$ *hlist*->**infoAnchor**;
>   Returns the *entryPath* of the current anchor.

$ *hlist*->**infoBbox**(*entryPath*);
>   Returns a list of four numbers describing the visible
>   bounding box of *entryPath.*

$ *hlist*->**infoChildren**(*?entryPath?*);
>   If *entryPath* is given, returns a list of its children entries,
>   otherwise returns a list of the toplevel.

$hlist->**infoData**(*?entryPath?*);
>   Returns the data associated with *entryPath*.

$hlist->**infoDragsite**;
>   Returns the *entryPath* of the current dragsite.

$hlist->**infoDropsite**;
>   Returns the *entryPath* of the current dropsite.

$hlist->**infoExists**(*entryPath*);
>   Returns a boolean value indicating whether *entryPath* exists.

$hlist->**infoHidden**(*entryPath*);
>   Returns a boolean value indicating whether *entryPath* is hidden.

$hlist->**infoNext**(*entryPath*);
>   Returns the *entryPath* of the list entry immediately below this list entry.

$hlist->**infoParent**(*entryPath*);
>   Returns the name of the parent of *entryPath*.

$hlist->**infoPrev**(*entryPath*);
>   Returns the *entryPath* of the list entry immediately above this list entry.

$hlist->**infoSelection**;
>   Returns a list of selected entries.

$hlist->**itemCget**(*entryPath, col, option*);
>   Returns the current value of *option* for *entryPath* at column *col*.

$hlist->**itemConfigure**(*entryPath, col, ?, option?, => ?value*);
>   Queries or modifies the configuration options of *entryPath* at column *col*.

$hlist->**itemCreate**(*entryPath, col, ?, -itemtype => type? ?, option => value*);
>   Creates a new display item at column *col* of *entryPath*.

$hlist->**itemDelete**(*entryPath, col*);
>   Deletes the display item at column *col* of *entryPath*.

$ *hlist*->**itemExists**(*entryPath, col*);
> Returns true if there is a display item at column *col* of *entryPath*.

$ *hlist*->**nearest**(*y*);
> Returns the *entryPath* of the visible element nearest to y-coordinate *y*.

$ *hlist*->**see**(*entryPath*);
> Adjusts the view so that *entryPath* is visible.

$ *hlist*->**selectionClear**(*?from? ?, to?*);
> Deselects the list entries *from* through *to*, inclusive.

$ *hlist*->**selectionGet**;
> This is an alias for the **infoSelection** widget command.

$ *hlist*->**selectionIncludes**(*entryPath*);
> Returns true if *entryPath* is currently selected.

$ *hlist*->**selectionSet**(*from ?, to ?*);
> Selects each list entry(s) between *from* and *to*, inclusive.

$ *hlist*->**showEntry**(*?entryPath?*);
> Shows the list entry *entryPath*.

$ *hlist*->**xview**;
> Returns a list of two real fractions between 0 and 1 describing the horizontal span that is visible in the window.

$ *hlist*->**xview**(*entryPath*);
> Adjusts the view in the window so that the list entry identified by *entryPath* is aligned to the left edge of the window.

$ *hlist*->**xviewMoveto**(*fraction*);
> Adjusts the view in the window so that *fraction* of the total width of the HList is off-screen to the left.

$ *hlist*->**xviewScroll**(*int,* units | pages);
> Shifts the view in the window left or right *int* characters or screens.

$blist->**yview**;

> Returns a list of real fractions between 0 and 1 describing the vertical span that is visible in the window.

$blist->**yview**(*entryPath*);

> Adjusts the view in the window so that *entryPath* is displayed at the top of the window.

$blist->**yviewMoveto**(*fraction*);

> Adjusts the view in the window so that *fraction* of the total height of the HList is off-screen to the top.

$blist->**yviewScroll**(*int,* units | pages);

> Shifts the view in the window up or down *int* lines or screens.

LabFrame

LabFrame is a frame with a label, on either side, top, or bottom.

```
-borderwidth              -highlightthickness
-cursor                   -relief
-height                   -takefocus
-highlightbackground      -width
-highlightcolor
```

-label => *labelString*

> The text of the label to be placed with the Frame.

-labelside => *side*

> One of left, right, top, bottom, or acrosstop.

NoteBook

NoteBook displays several windows in limited space. The notebook is divided into a stack of pages of which only one is displayed at any time. The other pages can be selected by means of choosing the visual *tabs* at the top of the widget.

```
-borderwidth              -highlightthickness
-cursor                   -relief
-height                   -takefocus
```

```
-highlightbackground        -width
-highlightcolor
```

-dynamicgeometry => *boolean*
> False ensures all noteboook pages are the same size. True resizes the notebook as different pages are selected.

-ipadx => *pixels*
> The amount of internal horizontal padding around the pages.

-ipady => *pixels*
> The amount of internal vertical padding around the pages.

$note->**add**(*page, -option => value*);
> Adds a page with name *page* to the notebook. *-option* may be:

> -anchor => n | ne | e | se | s | sw | w | nw | center
>> Specifies how the information in a tab is to be displayed.

> -bitmap => *bitmap*
>> Specifies a bitmap to display on the tab of this page. The bitmap is displayed only if none of the -label or -image options are specified.

> -image => *image*
>> Specifies an image to display on the tab of this page. The image is displayed only if the -label option is not specified.

> -label => *string*
>> Specifies the text string to display on the tab of this page.

> -justify => left | right | center
>> When there are multiple lines of text displayed in a tab, this option determines the justification of the lines.

> -createcmd => *callback*
>> The *callback* invoked the first time the page is shown on the screen.

-raisecmd => *callback*
> The *callback* invoked whenever this page is raised by the user.

-state => normal|disabled
> Specifies whether this page can be raised by the user.

-underline => *integer*
> Specifies the integer index of a character to underline in the tab.

-wraplength => *integer*
> This option specifies the maximum line length of the label string on this tab.

$ *note*->**delete**(*page*);
> Deletes the page identified by *page*.

$ *note*->**pagecget**(*page*, *-option*);
> Returns the current value of the configuration option given by *-option* in the page given by *page*. Options may have any of the values accepted in the **add** method.

$ *note*->**pageconfigure**(*page*, *-option* => *value*);
> Like configure for the page indicated by *page*. Options may be any of the options accepted by the **add** method.

$ *note*->**raise**(*page*);
> Raises the page identified by *page*.

$ *note*->**raised**;
> Returns the name of the currently raised page.

Optionmenu

The Optionmenu widget allows the user to choose between a given set of options using a pulldown list.

-activebackground	-highlightthickness
-activeforeground	-image
-anchor	-justify
-background	-padx
-bitmap	-pady
-borderwidth	-relief

```
-cursor                    -state
-disabledforeground        -takefocus
-font                      -text
-foreground                -textvariable
-height                    -underline
-highlightbackground       -width
-highlightcolor            -wraplength
```

-options => [*optionList*]
> The menuitems, specified as a reference to a list of strings.

-command => *callback*
> The *callback* to invoke after *varRef* of -textvariable is set.

ROText

This is a Text widget with all bindings removed that would alter the contents of the text widget. Text can be inserted programmatically but not altered by the user.

Scrolled

Perl/Tk includes the special constructor **Scrolled** which creates a widget with attached scrollbars, as long as the widget class supports the x/y scrollcommand(s), as Canvas, Entry, Listbox, and Text do. Scrollbars can be required, or might spring into existence only when needed.

> $*scrolled* = $*parent*->**Scrolled**(*widgetClass* …);

You may specifiy option/value pairs which are passed to the *widgetClass* constructor.

-scrollbars => *scrollbarSpecs*
> The strings n, s, e, and w specifiy top, bottom, left, or right scrollbars, respectively. The string *sw* creates two scrollbars on the left and bottom of the widget. The string o means optional and r required, so rwos means required on west (vertical), optional on south (horizontal).

TixGrid

This widget displays its contents in a two-dimensional grid of
cells. Each cell may contain one Tix display item, which may
be in text, graphics, or other formats. Individual cells, or
groups of cells, can be formatted with a wide range of
attributes, such as color, relief, and border.

```
-background            -pady
-borderwidth           -relief
-cursor                -selectbackground
-exportselection       -selectborderwidth
-font                  -selectforeground
-foreground            -state
-height                -takefocus
-highlightbackground   -width
-highlightcolor        -xscrollcommand
-highlightthickness    -yscrollcommand
-padx
```

-browsecmd => *callback*

Invokes the *callback* with the selected entry when it's
browsed. The *callback* is passed two additional parameters: *x* and *y*, the location of the cell.

-command => *callback*

Invokes the *callback* with the selected entry when it's
activated.

-editdonecmd => *callback*

Invokes the *callback* with the selected entry when it's
edited. The *callback* is passed two additional parameters:
x and *y*, the location of the cell.

-editnotifycmd => *callback*

Invokes the *callback* with the selected entry when an
attempt is made to edit a cell. The *callback* is passed two
additional parameters: *x* and *y*, the location of the cell.
Return *true* if the cell is editable.

-floatingcols => *integer*

Number of columns that are fixed when the widget is hor-
izontally scrolled. These columns can be used as labels for

the columns. The floating columns can be configured in the -formatcmd callback with the **formatBorder** method. The default value is 0.

-floatingrows => *integer*
> Number of rows that are fixed when the widget is vertically scrolled. These rows can be used as labels for the rows. The floating rows can be configured in the -formatcmd callback with the **formatBorder** method. The default value is 0.

-formatcmd => *callback*
> Invokes the *callback* when grid cells need formatting. Five parameters are supplied: *type, x1, y1, x2, y2. type* gives the logical type of the region of the grid, and may be:

> *x-region*
>> The horizontal margin.

> *y-region*
>> The vertical margin.

> *s-region*
>> The area where the horizontal and vertical margins are joined.

> *main*
>> Cells that do not fall into the above three types.

x1, y1, x2, y2
> The extent of the region that needs formatting.

-leftmargin => *integer*
> The width of the vertical margin (0 for no margin).

-itemtype => *itemType*
> text| textimage| window.

-selectmode => *mode*
> single (default), browse| multiple| extended.

-selectunit => *unit*
> cell| column| row.

-sizecmd => *callback*
    Invokes *callback* when grid resizes.

-topmargin => *integer*
    The height of the horizontal margin (0 for no margin).

$ *tixgrid*->**anchorClear**;
    Clears the anchor cell.

$ *tixgrid*->**anchorGet**(*x, y*);
    Returns the coordinates of the anchor cell.

$ *tixgrid*->**anchorSet**(*x, y*);
    Sets the coordinates of the anchor cell.

$ *tixgrid*->**bdtype**(*x, y* ?, *xbdWidth, ybdWidth*?);

$ *tixgrid*->**deleteColumn**(*from* ?, *to*?);
    Deletes columns specified by *from* and *to* inclusively.

$ *tixgrid*->**deleteRow**(*from* ?, *to*?);
    Deletes rows specified by *from* and *to* inclusively.

$ *tixgrid*->**dragsite**(*option, x, y*);
    Not implemented.

$ *tixgrid*->**dropsite**(*option, x, y*);
    Not implemented.

$ *tixgrid*->**editApply**;
    If any cell is being edited, de-highlights the cell and
    applies the changes.

$ *tixgrid*->**editSet**(*x, y*);
    Highlights the cell at (*x, y*) for editing if the *-editnotify*
    callback returns true for this cell.

$ *tixgrid*->**entrycget**(*x, y, -option*);
    Returns the current value of the configuration option
    given by *-option* of the cell at (*x, y*).

$ *tixgrid*->**entryconfigure**(*x, y* ?, *-option*? ?=> *value*?);
    Queries or modifies the configuration options of the cell
    at (*x, y*).

$tixgrid->**formatBorder**(*x1, y1, x2, y2, options*);

$tixgrid->**formatGrid**(*x1, y1, x2, y2, options*);
> **format** can only be called by the *-formatcmd* callback.

$tixgrid->**geometryinfo**(*?width? ?, height?*);
> Returns a list of 4 floats describing diagonal corners of a rectangle.

$tixgrid->**index**(*x, y*);
> Returns (*nx, ny*) of entry at position (*x, y*).

$tixgrid->**info**(*option ?, args?*);

$tixgrid->**moveColumn**(*from, to, offset*);
> Moves columns specified by *from* and *to* according to the amount of *offset*.

$tixgrid->**moveRow**(*from, to, offset*);
> Moves rows specified by *from* and *to* according to the amount of *offset*.

$tixgrid->**nearest**(*x, y*);
> Returns the pixel position of the grid cell at (*x, y*).

$tixgrid->**selectionAdjust**(*x1, y1 ?, x2, y2?*);

$tixgrid->**selectionClear**(*x1, y1 ?, x2, y2?*);

$tixgrid->**selectionIncludes**(*x1, y1 ?, x2, y2?*);

$tixgrid->**selectionSet**(*x1, y1 ?, x2, y2?*);

$tixgrid->**selectionToggle**(*x1, y1 ?, x2, y2?*);

$tixgrid->**set**(*x, y ?, -itemtype => type? ?, -option => value?*);
> Creates a new display item at cell (*x, y*). *-itemtype* gives the type of the display item.

$tixgrid->**sizeColumn**(*index ?, -option? ?=>value?*);
> See **sizeRow**.

$tixgrid->**sizeRow**(*index ?, -option? ?=> value?*);
> Queries or sets the size of the row or column given by *index*. *Index* can be a positive intetger the string *default*. *-option* may be one of the following:

-pad0 => pixels
> Specifies the paddings to the left of a column or the top of a row.

-pad1 => pixels
> Specifies the paddings to the right of a column or the bottom of a row.

-size => val
> May be *auto,* a screen size, or a float followed by the string *chars.*

$*tixgrid*->**sort**(*dimension, start, end, ?args …?*);

$*tixgrid*->**unset**(*x, y*);
> Removes the display items at cell (*x, y*).

$*tixgrid*->**xview**;

$*tixgrid*->**yview**;

TList

TList is used to display data in a tabular format. TList extends the plain listbox widget because list entries can be displayed in a two dimensional format. Graphical images as well as multiple colors and fonts can be used for the list entries.

```
-background           -relief
-borderwidth          -selectbackground
-cursor               -selectborderwidth
-exportselection      -selectforeground
-font                 -setgrid
-foreground           -takefocus
-height               -width
-highlightbackground  -xscrollcommand
-highlightcolor       -yscrollcommand
-highlightthickness
```

-browsecmd => callback
> Invokes the *callback* with the selected entry when it's browsed.

`-command => `*`callback`*

Invokes the *callback* with the selected entry when it's activated.

`-itemtype => `*`displayStyle`*

Specifies the default type of display item for this TList widget. When you call the insert methods, display items of this type will be created if the `-itemtype` option is not specified.

`-orient => vertical|horizontal`

Specifies the order of tabularizing the list entries.

`-padx => `*`width`*

The default horizontal padding for list entries.

`-pady => `*`height`*

The default vertical padding for list entries.

`-selectbackground => `*`color`*

Specifies the background color for the selected list entries.

`-selectborderwidth => `*`width`*

Specifies a non-negative value indicating the width of the 3-D border to draw around selected items.

`-selectforeground => `*`color`*

Specifies the foreground color for the selected list entries.

`-selectmode => `*`mode`*

Specifies one of several styles for manipulating the selection, either `single`, `browse`, `multiple`, or `extended`; the default is `single`.

`-sizecmd => `*`callback`*

Specifies a *callback* that's invoked when the widget changes size.

`-state => normal|disabled`

Specifies whether the TList command should react to user actions. When set to `normal`, the TList reacts to user actions in the normal way. When set to `disabled`, the TList can only be scrolled, but its entries cannot be selected or activated.

Listbox Indices:

>*number* (starts at 0), `active`, `anchor`, `end`, `@x, y`

$*tlist*->**anchorSet**(*index*);
> Sets the anchor to the list entry identified by *index*.

$*tlist*->**anchorClear**;
> Removes the anchor, if any, from this TList widget.

$*tlist*->**delete**(*from* ?, *to*?);
> Deletes one or more list entries between the two entries
> specified by the indices *from* and *to*.

$*tlist*->**dragsiteSet**(*index*);
> Not implemented.

$*tlist*->**dragsiteClear**;
> Not implemented.

$*tlist*->**dropsiteSet**(*index*);
> Not implemented.

$*tlist*->**dropsiteClear**;
> Not implemented.

$*tlist*->**entrycget**(*index, -option*);
> Returns the current value of the configuration option
> given by *-option* for the entry identified by *index*.

$*tlist*->**entryconfigure**(*index* ?, *-option, ?value*?);
> Query or modify the configuration options of the list entry
> identified by *index*.

$*tlist*->**infoAnchor**(*index*);
> Returns the *index* of the current anchor, if any, else
> returns the empty string.

$*tlist*->**infoDragsite**(*dragsite, index*);
> Returns the *index* of the current *dragsite*, if any, else
> returns the empty string.

$*tlist*->**infoDropsite**(*dropsite, index*);
> Returns the *index* of the current *dropsite*, if any, else
> returns the empty string.

$tlist->**infoSelection**;

Returns a list of selected elements in the TList widget, else returns an empty string.

$tlist->**insert**(*index* ?, -*option* => *value*?);

Creates a new list entry at the position indicated by *index*. The following configuration options can be given to configure the list entry:

-itemtype => *displayStyle*

Specifies the type of display item, one of image | imagetext | text | window.

-state => *state*

Specifies whether this entry can be selected or invoked by the user—normal | disabled.

$tlist->**nearest**(*x, y*);

Given an (x, y) coordinate within the TList window, returns the index of the element nearest to that coordinate.

$tlist->**see**(*index*);

Adjusts the view in the TList so that the entry given by *index* is visible.

$tlist->**selectionClear**(?*from*?, ?*to*?);

Deselects the specified entries in the TList widget.

$tlist->**selectionIncludes**(*index*);

Returns 1 if the list entry indicated by *index* is currently selected, else 0.

$tlist->**selectionSet**(*from* ?, *to*?);

Selects each list entry between *from* and *to*, inclusive, without affecting the selection state of entries outside that range.

$tlist->**xview**;

Returns a list containing two elements. Each element is a real fraction between 0 and 1; together they describe the horizontal span that is visible in the window.

$tlist->**xview**(*index*);

> Adjusts the view in the window so that the list entry identified by *index* is aligned to the left edge of the window.

$tlist->**xviewMoveto**(*float*);

> Adjusts the view in the window so that *float* of the total width of the TList is off-screen to the left. *float* must be between 0 and 1.

$tlist->**xviewScroll**(*integer, what*);

> Shifts the view in the window left or right according to *integer* and *what*. *what* must be either `units` or `pages`.

$tlist->**yview**;

> Returns a list containing two elements. Each element is a real fraction between 0 and 1; together they describe the vertical span that is visible in the window.

$tlist->**yview**(*index*);

> Adjusts the view in the window so that the list entry given by *index* is displayed at the top of the window.

$tlist->**yviewMoveto**(*float*);

> Adjusts the view in the window so that the list entry given by *float* appears at the top of the window. *float* must be between 0 and 1.

$tlist->**yviewScroll**(*integer, what*);

> Shifts the view in the window up or down according to *integer* and *what*. *what* must be either `units` or `pages`.

Tree

A Tree widget is derived from the HList class and inherits all its commands, options, and subwidgets. Tree displays hierachical data in a tree form, adjustable by opening or closing parts of the tree.

```
-background              -relief
-borderwidth             -selectbackground
-cursor                  -selectborderwidth
-exportselection         -selectforeground
-font                    -setgrid
```

```
-foreground                    -takefocus
-height                        -width
-highlightbackground           -xscrollcommand
-highlightcolor                -yscrollcommand
-highlightthickness
```

-browsecmd => *callback*

Invokes the *callback* with the selected entry when it's browsed.

-closecmd => *callback*

Invokes the *callback* with the selected entry when it's closed.

-command => *callback*

Invokes the *callback* with the selected entry when it's activated.

-ignoreinvoke => *boolean*

Specifies whether or not a branch should be opened or closed when (+) or (-) is selected.

-opencmd => *callback*

Invokes the *callback* with the selected entry when it's opened.

$*tree*->**autosetmode**;

Sets mode of Tree widget entries: 'none' if an entry has no child entries, 'open' if an entry has hidden child entries, else 'close'.

$*tree*->**close**(*entryPath*);

Closes the entry given by *entryPath* if its mode is close.

$*tree*->**getmode**(*entryPatch*);

Returns the current mode of the entry given by entryPath.

$*tree*->**open**(*entryPath*);

Opens the entry given by *entryPath* if its mode is open.

$*tree*->**setmode**(*entryPath* => *mode*);

Sets *entryPath* to open, close, or none.

Other Perl/Tk Widgets

Here are lesser known widgets from the Perl/Tk distribution (most have POD documentation):

Form   A geometry manager based on attachment rules.

InputO   An invisible input only window that accepts user input via bindings.

Table   A geometry manager that displays a two dimensional table of arbitrary Perl/Tk widgets.

Tiler   Similar to Table.

For information on more user-contributed widgets visit the Perl/Tk home page at *http://www.connect.net/gbarr/PerlTk*.

Display Items
and Display Styles

ImageText Display Items

Display items of type *imagetext* display an image together with a text string. Imagetext items support the following options:

`-bitmap` => *bitmap*
> Specifies the bitmap to display in the item.

`-image` => *image*
> Specifies the image to display in the item. When both the `-bitmap` and `-image` options are specified, only the image is displayed.

`-style` => *itemStyle*
> Specifies the *itemstyle* to use for this item. Must be the name of an *imagetext* style created with **ItemStyle**.

`-showimage` => *boolean*
> A boolean value that specifies whether the image/bitmap should be displayed.

`-showtext => `*boolean*

A boolean value that specifies whether the text string should be displayed.

`-text => `*string*

Specifies the text *string* to display in the item.

`-underline => `*integer*

Specifies the index of a character to underline in the text string (0 is the first character).

ImageText item style options:

`-activebackground`	`-font`
`-activeforeground`	`-justify`
`-anchor`	`-padx`
`-background`	`-pady`
`-disabledbackground`	`-selectbackground`
`-disabledforeground`	`-selectforeground`
`-foreground`	`-wraplength`

`-gap => `*integer*

Specifies the distance between the bitmap/image and the text string, in pixels.

Text Display Items

Display items of the type *text* display a text string. Text items support the following options:

`-style => `*itemStyle*

Specifies the *itemStyle* to use for this text item. Must be the name of a *text* style created with **ItemStyle**.

`-text => `*string*

Specifies the text *string* to display in the item.

`-underline => `*integer*

Specifies the index of a character to underline in the text string (0 is the first character).

Text item style options:

`-activebackground`	`-font`
`-activeforeground`	`-justify`

```
-anchor                    -padx
-background                -pady
-disabledbackground        -selectbackground
-disabledforeground        -selectforeground
-foreground                -wraplength
```

Window Display Items

Display items of the type *window* display a Perl/TK widget.
Window items support the following options:

`-style =>` *itemStyle*

>Specifies the *itemStyle* to use for this window item.
>Must be the name of a widget display style created with
>**ItemStyle**.

`-widget =>` *widgetRef*

>Specifies the widget to display in the item.

Window item style options:

`-anchor`   `-padx`   `-pady`

Creating and Manipulating Item Styles

$widget->ItemStyle(*itemType,* `?-`stylename `=>` *name?,*
`?-`refwindow `=>` *widgetRef?,* `?-option =>` *value?*);

>*itemType* is an existing display item type, a widget refer-
>ence or a new type added by the user. *-stylename* speci-
>fies a name for this style. *-refwindow* specifies a widget to
>use for determining the default values of the display type.
>If unspecified, $*widget* is used. Default values for the dis-
>play types can be set via the options database.

$style->delete;

>Destroy this display style object.

11. Composite and Derived Widgets

Composite and derived widgets are defined by a **package**.
Composites are generally made from a Frame or TopLevel

---

widget with *subwidgets* arranged inside. Derived widgets change the functionality of an existing widget.

```perl
package Tk::Frog;
use Tk:SomeWidget;
use base qw/Tk::Derived Tk::SomeWidget/;
Construct Tk::Widget 'Frog';

sub ClassInit{
  my($class, $mainwindow) = @_;

  # Initalize the new widget class.
  # Perhaps, define class bindings.

  $class->SUPER::ClassInit($mainwindow);
}

sub Populate {
  my($self, $args) = @_;

  # Use composite container $self and populate
  # it with subwidgets. $args is a reference
  # to a hash of option/value pairs.

  my $option = delete $args->{-option};
  $self->SUPER::Populate($args);
  $self->Advertise();
  $self->Callback();
  $self->Component();
  $self->ConfigSpecs();
  $self->Delegates();
  $self->Subwidget();
}

1; # end class Frog
```

$*self*->**Advertise**(*subwidgetName* => $*subwidget*);
   Makes widget $*subwidget* visible outside the composite with name *subwidgetName* (see **Subwidget**).

$*self*->**Callback**(*-option* ?, *args*?);
   Executes the callback defined with $*self*->**ConfigSpecs** (*-option*, [CALLBACK, ...]); If *args* are given they are

passed to the callback. If *-option* is undefined it does nothing.

$*self*->**Component**(*widgetClass* => *subwidgetName*?, *-option* => *value*?);

Creates a widget of kind *widgetClass* with the specified option/value pairs and **Advertise** it with name *subwidget-Name*.

$*self*->**ConfigAlias**(*-alias* => *-option*);

Makes option *-alias* equivalent to *-option*.

$*self*->**ConfigSpecs**(*-option* => [*where, dbName, dbClass, fallback*]);

Defines **configure** option *-option* having the database name *dbName* and class *dbClass* with fallback value *fallback* (in case nothing is defined in the resource database). Multiple options can be specified. *where* can be:

ADVERTISED

Configure advertised subwidgets.

CALLBACK

Treat the option as a standard Perl/Tk callback and execute it by calling **Callback**.

CHILDREN

Configure children.

DESCENDANTS

Configure descendants.

METHOD

Invoke $*self*->*option*(*value*). Simply provide a class method with the same name as the option, minus the dash.

PASSIVE

Store option value in $*self*->{Configure}{*-option*}.

SELF

Configure the containing widget (**Frame** or **Toplevel**).

$subwidget

Invoke $subwidget->**configure**(-option => value)

$self -> **ConfigSpecs**(-option => [{-option1 => $w1, -option2 => [$w2, $w3]}, dbName, dbClass, fallback]);

So $self->configure(-option => value) actually does:

```
$w1->configure(-option1 => value);
$w2->configure(-option2 => value);
$w3->configure(-option2 => value);
```

$self->**ConfigSpecs**('DEFAULT' => [where]);

How to handle default **configure** requests.

$self->**Delegates**(methodName => $w1 ?, 'DEFAULT' => $w2?);

Redirect composite widget method methodName to subwidget $subwidget. Multiple method/widget pairs can be specified.

$self->**Subwidget**(subwidgetName);

Return the widget reference belonging to the advertised subwidget subwidgetName.

12. Images

Images are created using the **DefineBitmap**, **Bitmap**, and **Photo** methods, described below. Bitmaps have a pixel depth of 2 bits, whereas Photos can be full color 24 bit XPM, GIF, PPM or XBM objects.

$widget->**Getimage**(name);

Given name, look for an image file with that base name and return a Tk image object. File extensions are tried in this order: xpm, gif, ppm, xbm until a valid iamge is found. If no image is found, try a built-in image with that name.

$widget->**DefineBitmap**(bitmapName, bitColumns, bitRows, bitVector);

Define a bitmap named bitmapName directly in Perl code. The first bitColumns bits packed in bitVector are row one.

Here are image manipulation methods common to the remaining two image types:

$*image*->**delete**;
> Deletes the image.

$*image*->**height**;
> Returns pixel height of image.

$*image*->**imageNames**;
> Returns a list of the names of all existing images.

$*image*->**type**;
> Returns the type of image.

$*image*->**imageTypes**;
> Returns a list of valid image types.

$*image*->**width**;
> Returns pixel width of image.

When an image is created via the `DefineBitmap`, `Bitmap`, or `Photo` method, Tk creates an image object reference to the the image. For all image types, this object supports the **cget** and **configure** methods in the same manner as widgets for changing and querying configuration options. Of course, image configuration commands can still be passed to the creation method:

$*image* = $*mw*->**Photo**(*-file* => *'/home/bug/photo.gif'*);

The Bitmap Image Method

`-background` => *color*
> Set background color for bitmap.

`-data` => *string*
> Specify contents of bitmap in X11 bitmap format.

`-file` => *pathName*
> Gives name of file whose contents define the bitmap in X11 bitmap format.

`-foreground => ` *color*

> Set foreground color for bitmap.

`-maskdata => ` *string*

> Specify contents of mask in X11 bitmap format.

`-maskfile => ` *pathName*

> Gives name of file whose contents define the mask in X11 bitmap format.

The Photo Image Method

`-data => ` *string*

> Specifies contents of image in a supported format.

`-format => ` *formatName*

> Specifies format for data specified with the `-data` or `-file` options.

`-file => ` *pathName*

> Gives name of file whose contents define the image in supported format.

`-height => ` *number*

> Specifies pixel height of the image.

`-palette => ` *paletteSpec*

> Sets the resolution of the color cube to be allocated for image.

`-width => ` *number*

> Specifies pixel width of the image.

$ *image*->**blank**;

> Blanks the image so it has no data and is completely transparent.

$ *image*->**copy**(*sourceImage* ?, -*option* => *value* …?);

> Copies a region from *sourceImage* to $ *image* using given options.

> `-from => ` *x1, y1, x2, y2*

> > Specifies rectangular region of source image to be copied.

-to => *x1, y1, x2, y2*

    Specifies rectangular region of target image to be affected.

-shrink

    Clips target image so copied region is in bottom-right corner.

-zoom => *x, y*

    Magnifies source region by *x, y* in respective direction.

-subsample => *x, y*

    Reduces source image by using only every *x y*th pixel.

$image->**get**(*x, y*);

    Returns RGB value of pixel at coords *x, y* as list of three integers.

$image->**put**(*data* ?-to => *x1, y1, x2, y2*?);

    Sets pixels values for the region *x1, y1, x2, y2* for 2-D array *data*.

$image->**read**(*pathName* ?, -option => *value* ...?);

    Reads image data from file *pathName* into $*image* using given options.

-format => *format-name*

    Specifies image format of file.

-from => *x1, y1, x2, y2*

    Specifies a rectangular region of the image file to copy from.

-shrink

    Clips image so copied region is in bottom-right corner.

-to => *x, y*

    Specifies coords of the top-left corner in image to copy into.

$image->**redither**;

    Redithers the image.

$ *image*->**write**(*pathName* ?, *-option* => *value* …?);
   Writes image data from image into file *pathName*.

   -format => *format-name*
      Specifies image format for the file.

   -from => *x1, y1, x2, y2*
      Specifies a rectangular region of the image to copy
      from.

13. *Window Information*

$ *widget*->**atom**(*name*);
   Returns integer identifier for atom given by *name* on
   $ *widget*'s display.

$ *widget*->**atomname**(*id*);
   Returns textual name of atom given by integer *id* on
   $ *widget*'s display.

$ *widget*->**cells**;
   Returns number of cells in the colormap for $ *widget*.

$ *widget*->**children**;
   Returns a list containing widget references of all the children of $ *widget*.

$ *widget*->**class**;
   Returns the class name of $ *widget*.

$ *widget*->**colormapfull**;
   Returns 1 if the colormap for $ *widget* is full, 0 otherwise.

$ *widget*->**containing**(*rootX, rootY*);
   Returns the widget reference of window containing the
   point *rootX rootY* on $ *widget*'s display.

$ *widget*->**depth**;
   Returns the depth (bits per pixel) of $ *widget*.

Exists($ *widget*);
   Returns 1 if there exists a window for $ *widget*, ' ' (false) if
   no such window exists.

$widget->fpixels(number);
Returns floating-point value giving the number of pixels in *$widget* corresponding to the distance given by *number*.

$widget->geometry;
Returns the pixel geometry for *$widget*, in the form *widthxheight+x+y*.

$widget->height;
Returns height of *$widget* in pixels.

$widget->id;
Returns a hexadecimal string indicating the X identifier for *$widget*.

$widget->interps;
Returns a list of all Perl interpreters registered on *$widget*'s display.

$widget->ismapped;
Returns 1 if *$widget* is currently mapped, 0 otherwise.

$widget->MainWindow;
Returns a reference to *$widget*'s **MainWindow**.

$widget->manager;
Returns the name of the geometry manager currently responsible for *$widget*.

$widget->name;
Returns *$widget*'s name within its parent as opposed to its full pathname.

$widget->parent;
Returns the pathname of *$widget*'s parent.

$widget->PathName;
Returns *$widget*'s full pathname.

$widget->pathname(id);
Returns the widget reference of the window whose X identifier is *id* on *$widget*'s display.

$widget->**pixels**(*number*);

Returns the number of pixels in $widget corresponding to the distance given by *number*, rounded to the nearest integer.

$widget->**pointerx**;

Returns mouse pointer's x-coordinate on $widget's screen.

$widget->**pointerxy**;

Returns mouse pointer's x- and y-coordinates on $widget's screen.

$widget->**pointery**;

Returns mouse pointer's y-coordinate on $widget's screen.

$widget->**reqheight**;

Returns a decimal string giving $widget's requested height, in pixels.

$widget->**reqwidth**;

Returns a decimal string giving $widget's requested width, in pixels.

$widget->**rgb**(*color*);

Returns a list of the three RGB values that correspond to *color* in $widget.

$widget->**rootx**;

Returns the x-coordinate, in the root window of the screen, of the upper-left corner of $widget (including its border).

$widget->**rooty**;

Returns the y-coordinate, in the root window of the screen, of the upper-left corner of $widget (including its border).

$widget->**screen**;

Returns the name of the screen associated with $widget, in the form *displayName.screenIndex*.

$widget->**screencells**;

Returns the number of cells in the default color map for $widget's screen.

$widget->screendepth;

Returns the depth (bits per pixel) of $widget's screen.

$widget->screenheight;

Returns the height in pixels of $widget's screen.

$widget->screenmmheight;

Returns the height in millimeters of $widget's screen.

$widget->screenmmwidth;

Returns the width in millimeters of $widget's screen.

$widget->screenvisual;

Returns the visual class of $widget's screen. May be `directcolor`, `grayscale`, `pseudocolor`, `staticcolor`, `staticgray`, or `truecolor`.

$widget->screenwidth;

Returns the width in pixels of $widget's screen.

$widget->server;

Returns server information on $widget's display.

$widget->toplevel;

Returns the widget reference of the toplevel window containing $widget.

$widget->viewable;

Returns 1 if $widget and all of its ancestors up through the nearest toplevel window are mapped. Returns 0 if any of these windows is not mapped.

$widget->visual;

Returns the visual class of $widget (see $widget-> screenvisual).

$widget->visualid;

Returns the X identifier for the visual for $widget.

$widget->visualsavailable;

Returns a list whose elements describe the visuals available for $widget's screen including class and depth.

$ *widget*->**vrootheight**;

    Returns the height of the virtual root window associated with $ *widget*.

$ *widget*->**vrootwidth**;

    Returns the width of the virtual root window associated with $ *widget*.

$ *widget*->**vrootx**;

    Returns the x-offset of the virtual root window associated with $ *widget*.

$ *widget*->**vrooty**;

    Returns the y-offset of the virtual root window associated with $ *widget*.

$ *widget*->**width**;

    Returns $ *widget*'s width in pixels.

$ *widget*->**x**;

    Returns x-coordinate, in $ *widget*'s parent, of the upper-left corner of $ *widget*.

$ *widget*->**y**;

    Returns y-coordinate, in $ *widget*'s parent, of the upper-left corner of $ *widget*.

14. The Window Manager

Many of the following methods have one or more optional arguments which, when specified, set something, but when missing, get something. The widget is typically a MainWindow or a Toplevel.

$ *mw*->**aspect**(?*minNumer, minDenom, maxNumer, maxDenom*?);

    Informs window manager of desired aspect ratio range for $ *mw*.

$ *mw*->**client**(?*name*?);

    Stores *name* in $ *mw*'s **WM_CLIENT_MACHINE** property. Informs window manager of client machine on which the application is running.

$ mw->colormapwindows(?*windowList*?);
Stores *windowList* in $ *mw*'s **WM_COLORMAP_WINDOWS**
property which identifies the internal windows within
$ *mw* with private colormaps.

$ mw->command(?*value*?);
Stores *value* in $ *mw*'s **WM_COMMAND** property.
Informs window manager of command used to invoke
the application.

$ mw->deiconify;
Arranges for $ *mw* to be mapped on the screen.

$ mw->focusmodel(?active | passive?);
Specifies the focus model for $ *mw*.

$ mw->frame;
Returns the X window identifier for the outermost deco-
rative frame containing $ *mw*. If $ *mw* has none, returns X
id of $ *mw* itself.

$ mw->geometry(?*newGeometry*?);
Changes geometry of $ *mw* to *newGeometry*. The form of
newGeometry is *width*x*height+x+y*.

$ mw->grid(?*baseWidth, baseHeight, widthInc, heightInc*?);
Indicates that $ *mw* is to be managed as a gridded window
with the specified relation between grid and pixel units.

$ mw->group(?*widgetRef*?);
Gives widget reference for leader of group to which $ *mw*
belongs.

$ mw->iconbitmap(?*bitmap*?);
Specifies a bitmap to use as icon image when $ *mw* is
iconified.

$ mw->iconify;
Arranges for $ *mw* to be iconfied.

$ mw->iconmask(?*bitmap*?);
Specifies a bitmap to use to mask icon image when $ *mw*
is iconified.

$mw->iconname(?*newName*?);
>   Specifies name to use as a label for $mw's icon.

$mw->iconposition(?*x, y*?);
>   Specifies position on root window to place $mw's icon.

$mw->iconwindow(?*widgetRef*?);
>   Sets widget reference of window to use as the icon when $mw is iconified.

$mw->maxsize(?*width, height*?);
>   Specifies maximum size $mw may be resized in each direction.

$mw->minsize(?*width, height*?);
>   Specifies minimum size $mw may be resized in each direction.

$mw->overrideredirect(?*boolean*?);
>   Sets or unsets the override-redirect flag of $mw commonly used by window manager to determine whether window should have a decorative frame.

$mw->positionfrom(?program | user?);
>   Indicates from whom the $mw's current position was requested.

$mw->protocol(?*name*? ?, *callback*?);
>   Specifies a Perl callback to be invoked for messages of protocol *name*.

$mw->resizable(?*widthBoolean, heightBoolean*?);
>   Specifies whether $mw's width and/or height is resizable.

$mw->sizefrom(?program | user?);
>   Indicates from whom the $mw's current size was requested.

$mw->state;
>   Returns current state of $mw: normal, iconic, or withdrawn.

$mw->title(?*string*?);
>   Sets title for $mw's decorative frame to *string*.

$ *mw*->**transient**(*?master?*);

Informs window manager that $ *mw* is a transient of the window *master*.

$ *mw*->**withdraw**;

Arranges for $ *mw* to be withdrawn from the screen.

15. Bindings and Virtual Events

Note that **bind** *callbacks* are implicitly passed the bound object as the first argument of the parameter list.

An *eventDescriptor* is a list of one or more event patterns. An event pattern may be a single character, a string of the form '<*modifier-modifier-type-detail*>', or '<<*name*>>' (a virtual event).

$ *widget*->**bind**;

Returns list of all *eventDescriptor*s for which a binding exists for $ *widget*.

$ *widget*->**bind**(*tag*);

Returns list of all *eventDescriptor*s for which a binding exists for *tag*.

$ *widget*->**bind**(*eventDescriptor*);

Returns the callback bound to the given *eventDescriptor* for $ *widget*.

$ *widget*->**bind**(*tag, eventDescriptor*);

Returns the callback bound to the given *eventDescriptor* for *tag*.

$ *widget*->**bind**(*eventDescriptor => callback*);

Binds *callback* to the given *eventDescriptor* for $ *widget*

$ *widget*->**bind**(*tag, eventDescriptor => callback*);

Binds *callback* to the given *eventDescriptor* for *tag*

$ *widget*->**bindtags**(*?tagList?*);

Sets the current precedence order of tags for $ *widget* to *tagList*. By default a Perl/Tk widget's *taglist* is *class,* instance, *toplevel*, all. Note that this ordering differs from that of Tcl/Tk's *instance, class, toplevel*, all.

$*widget*->**eventAdd**(*'<<virtual>>'*, *eventDescriptor* ?, *eventDescriptor*?);

Arranges for virtual event '*<<virtual>>*' to be triggered when any one of given *eventDescriptors* occur.

$*widget*->**eventDelete**(*'<<virtual>>'*?, *eventDescriptor*?);

Deletes given *eventDescriptors* (or all if none given) from list that triggers the virtual event '*<<virtual>>*'.

$*widget*->**eventGenerate**(*event* ?, -when => *when*? ?, -*option* => *value*);

Generate *event* in *widget*'s window as if it came from window system. Possible options are listed in the **Event Field** table below. The -when option sets when the event will be processed. Possible values for *when* are:

now	process immediately (default)
tail	place at end of event queue
head	place at beginning of event queue
mark	same as head but behind previous generated events

$*widget*->**eventInfo**(?'*<<virtual>>*'?);

Returns list of *eventDescriptors* that trigger virtual event '*<<virtual>>*' (if not given, returns list of defined virtual events).

Modifiers:

Any	Button1, B1	Mod1, M1
Control	Button2, B2	Mod2, M2
Shift	Button3, B3	Mod3, M3
Lock	Button4, B4	Mod4, M4
Double	Button5, B5	Mod5, M5
Triple	Meta, M	Alt

Types:

Activate	FocusOut
ButtonPress, Button	Gravity
ButtonRelease	KeyPress, Key
Circulate	KeyRelease
Colormap	Motion
Configure	Leave
Deactivate	Map
Destroy	Property
Enter	Reparent
Expose	Unmap
FocusIn	Visibility

Details: for buttons, a number 1-5
for keys, a keysym (/usr/include/X11/keysymdef.h)

Tags: widget instance (applies to just that window)
toplevel window (applies to all its internal windows)
class name (applies to all widgets in class)
all (applies to all windows)

Table 1: Event Fields

eventGenerate() Option	Code	Valid Events
-above => *window*	a	Configure
-borderwidth => *size*	B	Configure
-button => *number*	b	ButtonPress, ButtonRelease
-count => *number*	c	Expose
-detail => *detail*	d	Enter, Leave, Focus
-focus => *boolean*	f	Enter, Leave
-height => *size*	h	Configure
-keycode => *number*	k	KeyPress, KeyRelease
-keysym => *name*	K	KeyPress, KeyRelease
-mode => *notify*	m	Enter, Leave, Focus
-override => *boolean*	o	Map, Reparent, Configure

Table 1: Event Fields (continued)

eventGenerate() Option	Code	Valid Events
-place => *where*	p	Circulate
-root => *window*	R	*
-rootx => *coord*	X	*
-rooty => *coord*	Y	*
-sendevent => *boolean*	E	*all events*
-serial => *number*	#	*all events*
-state => *state*	s	*all events*
-subwindow => *window*	S	*
-time => *integer*	t	*, Property
-x => *coord*	x	*, †
-y => *coord*	y	*, †

*KeyPress, KeyRelease, ButtonPress, ButtonRelease, Enter, Leave, Motion

†Expose, Configure, Gravity, Reparent

$*widget*->**break**;

Exit callback and short-circuit **bindtags** search.

$eventStructure = $*widget*->**XEvent**;

Fetches the X11 event structure. Calling $*eventStructure* -> *code*; returns the value of the X11 event field *code* (for *code* see above).

$eventStructure = **$Tk::event**;

A binding can localize the X11 event structure with **$Tk::event** rather than calling **XEvent**.

$eventField = **Ev**(*Code*);

Binding callbacks can use the **Ev**() construct as arguments to the callback. When the callback is triggered **Ev**(*code*) is replaced by the value of the X11 event field *code* (for *code* see above).

16. Geometry Management
The pack Command

$*widget*->**pack**(?-*option* => value);

Details how $widget should be managed by the packer.

```
-after => sibling          -ipady => pixels
-anchor => anchor          -padx => pixels
-before => sibling         -pady => pixels
-expand => boolean         -fill => none | x | y | both
-in => master              -side =>
                              top | bottom | left | right

-ipadx => pixels
```

$widget->**packForget**;
Unmanages the given slave.

$widget->**packInfo**;
Returns list containing current pack configuration.

$master->**packPropagate**(?boolean?);
Enables or disables propogation for the window $master.

$master->**packSlaves**;
Returns lists of slaves in the window $master.

The place Command

$widget->**place**(-option => value ?, -option => value ...?);
Details how $widget should be managed by the placer.

```
-anchor => anchor          -relx => location
-height => size            -rely => location
-in => master              -x => location
-width => size             -y => location
-relheight => size         -bordermode => inside | outside | ignore
-relwidth => size
```

$widget->**placeForget**;
Unmanages $widget.

$widget->**placeInfo**;
Returns list containing current place configuration of
$widget.

$master->**placeSlaves**;
Returns lists of slaves in the window $master.

The grid Command

$widget->**grid**(?-option => value ...?);
   Details how $widget should be managed by the gridder.

-column => *n*	-padx => *amount*
-columnspan => *n*	-pady => *amount*
-in => *other*	-row => *n*
-ipadx => *amount*	-rowspan => *n*
-ipady => *amount*	-sticky => ?n l s l e l w l n s l ew?

$master->**gridBbox**(*column, row*);
   Returns an *approximate* bounding box in pixels of space
   occupied by *column, row.*

$master->**gridColumnconfigure**(*column* ?, -minsize =>
   size? ?, -weight => *int*? ?, -pad => *int*?);
   Set/get minimum column size, relative column weight,
   and column padding.

$slave->**gridForget**;
   Removes (and unmaps) $slave from grid of its master.

$slave->**gridInfo**;
   Returns list describing configuration state of $slave.

$master->**gridLocation**(*x, y*);
   Returns column and row containing screen units *x, y* in
   $master. If *x, y* is outside grid, -1 is returned.

$master->**gridPropagate**(?boolean?);
   Set/get whether $master tries to resize its ancestor win-
   dows to fit grid.

$master->**gridRemove**(*slave* ?, *slave*?);
   Removes (and unmaps) each slave from grid remember-
   ing its configuration.

$master->**gridRowconfigure**(*row* ?, -minsize => *size*? ?,
   -weight => *int*? ?, -pad => *int*?);
   Set/get minimum row size, relative row weight, and row
   padding.

$ *master*->**gridSize**;
> Returns size of grid (in columns, then rows) for $ *master.*

$ *master*->**gridSlaves**(?-row => *row*? ?, -column => *column*?);
> With no options, a list of all slaves in $ *master* is returned.
> Otherwise, returns a list of slaves in specified row and/or
> column.

Grid Relative Placement

-      Increases columnspan of *slave* to the left.

x   Leave an empty column.

^   Extends the rowspan of *slave* above.

17. Fonts

$ *widget*->**fontActual**(*fontDesc* ?, -option?);
> Returns actual value for -*option* used by *fontDesc* on
> $ *widget*'s display. If -*option* is not given, the complete
> option/actual value list is returned.

$ *widget*->**fontConfigure**(*fontname* ?, -option ?, value??);
> Queries/sets font options for application-created font
> *fontname.*

$ *widget*->**fontCreate**(?*fontname* ?, -option, value??);
> Creates new application font *fontname* with given font
> options.

$ *widget*->**fontDelete**(*fontname* ?, fontname?);
> Deletes given application-created fonts.

$ *widget*->**fontFamilies**;
> Returns list of known font families defined on $ *widget*'s
> display.

$ *widget*->**fontMeasure**(*fontDesc, text*);
> Returns width in pixels used by *text* when rendered in
> *fontDesc* on $ *widget*'s display.

$widget->**fontMetrics**(*fontDesc* ?, *metric*?);
> Queries font metrics of *fontDesc* on $*widget*'s display
> where *metric* may be one of -ascent, -descent,
> -linespace, or -fixed. If *metric* is not given, the
> complete metric/value list is returned.

$widget->**fontNames**;
> Returns list of application created fonts.

Font Description:

1. *fontname*
   Name of font created by the application with
   fontCreate().

2. *systemfont*
   Name of platform-specific font interpreted by graphics
   server.

3. *family* ?, *size* ?, *style*??
   A Perl list with first element the name of a font family; the
   optional second element is desired size, and additional
   elements chosen from normal or bold, roman or italic,
   underline and overstrike.

4. *option* => *value* ?, -*option* => *value*?
   A Perl list of *option/value*s as valid for **fontCreate**().

Font Options:

-family => *name*	Font family (e.g., Courier, Times, Helvetica).
-size => *size*	Size in points (or pixels if negative).
-weight => *weight*	Either normal (default) or bold.
-slant => *slant*	Either roman (default) or italic.
-underline => *boolean*	Whether or not font is underlined.
-overstrike => *boolean*	Whether or not font is overstruck.

18. Other Perl/Tk Commands

$path = Tk->**findINC**(*component*);
> Returns absolute pathname of *component* in installed Tk hierarchy.

$soe = Tk::**timeofday**;
> Returns floating-point second of Unix epoch.

$*widget*->**after**(*ms* ?, *callback*?);
> Arranges for the *callback* to be run in *ms* milliseconds. If the *callback* is omitted the program sleeps for *ms* milliseconds.

$*widget*->**afterCancel**(*id* | *callback*);
> Cancels a previous **after** either by *id* or *callback*.

$*widget*->**afterIdle**(*callback*);
> Arranges for the *callback* to be run as soon as Tk is idle.

$*widget*->**afterInfo**(*id*);
> Returns information on event *callback id*. With no *id*, returns a list of all existing *callback id*s.

$*widget*->**appname**(?*newName*?);
> Sets the interpreter name of the application to *newName*.

$*widget*->**BackTrace**(*errorMessage*);
> Appends the string *errorMessage* to the list of trace back messages.

$*widget*->**bell**;
> Rings the X bell on $*widget*'s display.

$*widget*->**bisque**;
> Sets default color palette to old bisque scheme.

$*widget*->**Busy**(?*-recurse* =>*1*?);
> Changes cursor to a watch until **Unbusy** is called. If -recurse is true, descend the widget hierarchy and change all cursors.

catch {*script*};
> An **eval** wrapper that traps errors. The script is actually a Perl *block*.

$widget->**clipboardAppend**(?*-format* => *fmt*? ?, *-type* => *type*?, *data*);
  Appends *data* to clipboard on *widget*'s display.

$widget->**clipboardClear**;
  Claims ownership of clipboard on $*widget*'s display, clearing its contents.

$widget->**destroy**;
  Destroys the given window and its descendents.

DoOneEvent(*eventBits*);
  Processes Tk events described by *eventBits*, which may be DONT_WAIT, WINDOW_EVENTS, FILE_EVENTS, TIMER_EVENTS, IDLE_EVENTS and ALL_EVENTS. When passed ALL_EVENTS **DoOneEvent** processes events as they arise, and puts the application to sleep when no further events are outstanding. It first looks for an X or I/O event and, if found, calls the handler and returns. If there is no X or I/O event, it looks for a single timer event, invokes the callback, and returns. If no X, I/O or timer event is ready, any pending idle callbacks are executed. In all cases, **DoOneEvent** returns 1. When passed DONT_WAIT, **DoOneEvent** works as above except that it returns immediately with a value of 0 if there are no events to process.

$widget->**DoWhenIdle**(*callback*);
  Queues *callback* in the low priority idle event queue. *callback* is not canceled when $*widget* is destroyed.

Tk::**Error**($*widget, errorMessage, traceBackMessages*));
  Pushes *errorMessage* onto the list of *traceBackMessages*.

Exists($*widget*);
  Returns 1 if there exists a window for $*widget*, ' ' (false) if no such window exists.

$widget->**fileevent**(*fileHandle, operation* => *callback*);
  Invokes the *callback* when *fileHandle* is ready for *operation*. *operation* may be readable|writable.

$ *widget*->focus;
Sets focus window to $ *widget*.

$ *widget*->focusCurrent;
Returns focus window on $widget's display.

$ *widget*->focusFollowsMouse;
Changes focus model of application so focus follows the mouse pointer.

$ *widget*->focusForce;
Sets the input focus for $ *widget's* display to $ *widget* even if another application has it.

$ *widget*->focusLast;
Returns the window which most recently had focus and is a descendent of $ *widget's* toplevel.

$ *widget*->focusNext;
Returns the next window after $ *widget* in focus order.

$ *widget*->focusPrev;
Returns the previous window before $ *widget* in focus order.

$ *widget*->grab;
Sets a local grab on $ *widget*.

$ *widget*->grabCurrent;
Returns name of current grab window on $ *widget's* display. If $ *widget* is omitted, returns list of all windows grabbed by the application.

$ *widget*->grabGlobal;
Sets a global grab.

$ *widget*->grabRelease;
Releases grab on $ *widget*.

$ *widget*->grabStatus;
Returns none, local, or global to describe grab state of $ *widget*.

$ *widget*->idletasks;
Flushes the low priority idle events queue.

$widget->**lower**(*?belowThis?*);
> Places $widget below window *belowThis* in stacking order.

MainWindow->*new*;
> Returns a reference to the *MainWindow*, the top of the widget hierarchy.

MainLoop;
> The last logical statement in your application; this statement initiates X11 event processing.

$widget->**OnDestroy**(*callback*);
> The *callback* is invoked when $widget is destroyed. All widget data structures and methods are available, unlike a **<Destroy>** binding.

$widget->**optionAdd**(*pattern => value ?, priority?*);
> Adds option with *pattern value* at *priority* (0-100) to database.

$widget->**optionClear**
> Clears option database and reloads from user's Xdefaults.

$widget->**optionGet**(*name, class*);
> Obtains option value for $widget under *name* and *class* if present.

$widget->**optionReadfile**(*pathName ?, priority?*);
> Reads options from Xdefaults-style file into option database at *priority*.

$widget->**Popup**(*menu, x, y ?, entry?*);
> Posts popup *menu* so that *entry* is positioned at root coords *x, y*.

$widget->**raise**(*?aboveThis?*);
> Places $widget above window *aboveThis* in stacking order.

$widget->**repeat**(*ms => callback*);
> Repeats *callback* every *ms* milliseconds until cancelled.

$widget->**scaling**(?*float*?);
> Sets or queries the scaling factor for conversion between physical units and pixels. *float* is pixels per point (1/72 inch).

$widget->**selectionClear**(?*-selection* => *selection*?);
> Clears *selection* (default **PRIMARY**) on $widget's display.

$widget->**selectionGet**(?*-selection* => *selection*? ?,
-type => *type*?);
> Retrieves *selection* from $widget's *display* using representation *type*.

$widget->**selectionHandle**(?*-selection* => *sel*? ?, *-type* => *type*?
?, *-format* => *fmt*? , *win* => *callback*);
> Arranges for *callback* to be run whenever *sel* of *type* is owned by *win*.

$widget->**selectionOwn**(?*-selection* => *selection*? ?,
-command => *callback*?);
> Causes $widget to become new owner of *selection* and arranges for *command* to be run when $widget later loses the *selection*.

$widget->**selectionOwner**(?*-selection* => *selection*?);
> Returns path name of $widget which owns *selection* on $widget's display.

$widget->**send**(?-async? *interp* => *callback*);
> Executes *callback* in the Tk application *interp* on $widget's display. If -async is specified, the $widget->**send** command will return immediately.

> To receive commands from a foreign application define a subroutine **Tk::Receive**($widget, *commandString*). Run *commandString* with taint checks on and untaint the received data.

$widget->**setPalette**(*color*);
> Sets the default background color and compute other default colors.

$widget->**setPalette**(*name* => *color*?, *name* => *color* ...?);
Sets the default color for the named color options explicitly.

$widget->**Unbusy**;
Changes cursor from a watch to its previous value.

$widget->**update**;
Handles all pending X11 events.

$widget->**waitVariable**(*varRef*);
Pauses program until global variable *varRef* is modified.

$widget->**waitVisibility**;
Pauses program until $*widget*'s visibility has changed.

$widget->**waitWindow**;
Pauses program until $*widget* is destroyed.

Index

More Titles from O'Reilly

Perl

Learning Perl, 2nd Edition

By Randal L. Schwartz & Tom Christiansen
Foreword by Larry Wall
2nd Edition July 1997
302 pages, ISBN 1-56592-284-0

Mastering Algorithms with Perl

By Jon Orwant, Jarkko Hietaniemi &
John Macdonald
1st Edition August 1999
704 pages, ISBN 1-56592-398-7

Perl 5 Pocket Reference, 3rd Edition

By Johan Vromans
3rd Edition May 2000
96 pages, ISBN 0-596-00032-4

Mastering Regular Expressions

By Jeffrey E. F. Friedl
1st Edition January 1997
368 pages, ISBN 1-56592-257-3

Perl in a Nutshell

By Ellen Siever, Stephen Spainhour &
Nathan Patwardhan
1st Edition December 1998
674 pages, ISBN 1-56592-286-7

Perl Cookbook

By Tom Christiansen & Nathan Torkington
1st Edition August 1998
794 pages, ISBN 1-56592-243-3

CGI Programming with Perl, 2nd Edition

By Scott Guelich, Shishir Gundavaram,&
Gunther Birznieks
2nd Edition July 2000
470 pages, ISBN 1-56592-419-3

Advanced Perl Programming

By Sriram Srinivasan
1st Edition August 1997
434 pages, ISBN 1-56592-220-4

Web Programming